A History of Journalism in China

A HISTORY OF JOURNALISM IN CHINA

Volume 9

Edited by Fang Hanqi

SILKROAD PRESS

Singapore • Hong Kong • Beijing • Honolulu

Published by

Enrich Professional Publishing (S) Private Limited
16L, Enterprise Road,
Singapore 627660
Website: www.enrichprofessional.com
A Member of Enrich Culture Group Limited

Hong Kong Head Office:
2/F, Rays Industrial Building, 71 Hung To Road, Kwun Tong, Kowloon, Hong Kong, China

China Office:
Rm 1800, Building C, Central Valley, 16 Hai Dian Zhong Jie, Haidian District, Beijing, China

United States Office:
PO Box 30812, Honolulu, HI 96820, USA

English edition © 2014 by Enrich Professional Publishing (S) Private Limited
Chinese original edition © 2004 China Renmin University Press

Translated by Phoebe Poon

Edited by Glenn Griffith and Phoebe Poon

ISBN (Hardback)   978-981-4332-33-0
ISBN (ebook)   978-981-4339-22-3 (pdf)
                       978-981-4339-23-0 (epub)

This publication is designed to provide accurate and authoritative information in regard to the subject matter covered. It is sold with the understanding that the publisher is not engaged in rendering legal, accounting, or other professional service. If legal advice or other expert assistance is required, the services of a competent professional person should be sought.

Printed in Hong Kong with woodfree paper from Japan

Contents

Chapter 23   Journalism during the New Era of Socialist Modernization

(October 1976–1991).. 1

Notes 141

Index 145

23

Chapter

Journalism during the New Era of Socialist Modernization (October 1976–1991)

The smashing of the Gang of Four in the fall of 1976 and the change in Party policies after the Third Plenary Session of the 11th CPC Central Committee in December 1978 ushered in an unprecedented spring harvest of journalism in China. Although Party journalism had trodden a somewhat rugged path during 1976 and 1977, the period proved a milestone in discussions regarding the criterion of truth and the reestablishment of dialectical materialism. Lin Biao and the Gang of Four were thoroughly criticized for their anti-Party behavior and "ultra-leftism." Hot criticism against leftist journalism contributed to the emancipation of the mind, the righting of wrongs, the development of Socialist modernization, the strengthening of Socialist spiritual civilization, and the prevention of bourgeois liberalism. A new height was reached in the modernization of Party and private newspapers, news agencies, radio, television, photojournalism, documentaries, journalism organizations, journalism education, journalism research, and news communications, as well as in the reform of journalism in China.

The Struggling Development of Party Journalism after the Cultural Revolution

The fall of the anti-revolutionary Gang of Four in October 1976 symbolized the end of the 10-year Cultural Revolution. During the two years leading up to the convention of the 11th CPC Central Committee, Party cadres and the masses were fueled by revolutionary and reconstruction activities, going all out to expose the guilt of the anti-revolutionary groups of Lin and Jiang. The reorganization of the Party and rectification of unjust cases began alongside the restoration of industrial and agricultural production as well as scientific and cultural education. Despite this, the eradication of political and ideological chaos created during the Cultural Revolution, extended by the left-leaning ideology of Hua Guofeng during his tenure as President, was not without hassles. Not until the 11th CPC Central Committee in December 1978 were obstacles to the rectification of the Cultural Revolution and left-leaning ideologies overcome.

The difficulties lied in the anti-revolutionary groups' manipulation of the media as a tool of power usurpation during the Cultural Revolution, which resulted in devastating damage to the news industry. With the opening of the New Era, China's media, now basically returned to the hands of the trusted Party cadres, was challenged with two new missions: the criticism of leftist ideologies in order to propel Socialist modernization, and the reinstatement of the long-disrupted tradition of Party journalism.

While the development of Party journalism was not immune to the yet unfavorable political circumstances in the aftermath of the Cultural Revolution, positive signs were demonstrated thanks to the patronage of the older-generation proletarian revolutionists represented by Deng Xiaoping. The most remarkable was the discussion over the statement "practice is the sole criterion for testing truth" since May 1978, which laid a solid foundation for the convention of the historic 11th CPC Central Committee in terms of rallying support for Deng's clique, forecasting the eventual emancipation of the mind and rectification of wrongs.

The smashing of the anti-revolutionary groups of Lin Biao and Jiang Qing

On October 18, 1976, the CPC leadership made a proclamation throughout the Party about the smashing of the anti-revolutionary group of Jiang, kicking off a centrally-led mass movement against the Lin and Jiang groups. In this, the propagandist role of the news media was played to the full. At the same time, the political movement also initiated a tide of self-correction in the field of journalism.

The denunciation of power usurpation through manipulating the news media

During the Cultural Revolution, the anti-revolutionary groups of Lin and Jiang ascended to the top of state power through open and secret, moderate and violent means. An effective political tool, the news media had been under their tightest grip. This made the open and thorough denunciation of the anti-revolutionary manipulation of the news media a top priority of the CPC following the smashing of the Gang of Four.

The denunciation began with the criticism of an article signed Liang Xiao, titled "Always Follow the Practice of Chairman Mao." In mid-November 1976, the *Guangming Daily* (*Guangming ribao* 光明日報), *People's Liberation Army Daily* (*Jiefangjun bao* 解放軍報), and *People's Daily* (*Renmin ribao* 人民日報) each published an article to denounce the Gang for falsifying Chairman Mao's will, commenting that Liang's article was a declaration of anti-revolutionary mobilization on behalf of the Gang, a piece of solid evidence of their power usurpation, and a record of their failed attempts. Following the publication of these articles, the *People's Daily* issued an editorial on December 17, 1967, titled "A Ferocious Leap before Perishing," which made a systematic denunciation of the Gang's forging of Mao's will and seizure of power. As such, a journalistic war against the anti-revolutionary groups was embarked upon.

These marked the beginning of a series of articles against Lin's group and the Gang. On January 14, 1977 was the *People's Daily*'s publication of "The Political Direction of People's Broadcasting Must Not Be Distorted," an article from the Criticism Group of the Central Broadcasting Bureau against Yao Wenyuan, who turned the media into the Gang's tool of power usurpation. On March 25, 1977, the Xinhua News Agency (Xinhua) published the editorial "Denunciate the Gang of Four's Heinous Crime of Revolting Against the Party with News Pictures," listing the Gang's anti-Party schemes with a focus on their manipulation of photo journalism. Also targeting at Yao Wenyuan, the third issue of *Red Flag* (*Hongqi* 紅旗) in 1977 revealed Yao's control and forced publication of anti-Party articles in the magazine in "Record of Troublemaking, Failure, and Downfall" while clarifying conceptual questions misinterpreted by Lin Biao and the Gang. Later, on November 23, 1977, the Shanghai *Liberation Daily* (*Jiefang ribao* 解放日報) and *Wenhui Bao* 文匯報, which had long fell under the control of the Gang, both published an editorial titled "How the Gang of Four and Its Remnants Controlled the Two Shanghainese Papers for Advancing Their Anti-revolutionary Program" in condemnation of the Gang's manipulation.

The Gang's disruption of reports in commemoration of former Premier Zhou Enlai during their control of the mass media was rebuked as a crime. At the first anniversary of the death of Premier Zhou, which came after the fall of the Gang, scores of commemorative articles emerged, echoing public sentiment. The news documentary *Our Immortal Premier Zhou Enlai* (*Jing'ai de zhou'enlai zongli yongchuibuxiu* 敬愛的周恩來總理永垂不朽), which had been banned by the Gang, too, was remade and broadcast across the nation. On January 6, 1977, Xinhua issued the article "Unquenchable Radiance, Unbreakable Remembrance" against Yao Wenyuan's interference with the publication of commemorative stories about Premier Zhou. In reproach of the ban on television broadcasts of mourning activities, the Central Newsreel and Documentary Film Studio and Criticism Group of the Central Broadcasting Bureau, respectively, published "A War in Shooting Commemoratory Films for Premier Zhou" and "Premier Zhou Lives Forever in the Hearts of the Chinese Nationals and People around the World" on the same day. On January 9, the *People's Daily* joined the denunciation with the article "Love and Hatred of 800 Million People: *People's Daily* Revolutionary Comrades in Deep Remembrance of Premier Zhou."

On January 17, 1977 came the Mass Criticism Group of the Ministry of Transport's "An Anti-Revolutionary Farce," published in the *People's Daily*, which exposed the Gang's fabrication of charges against Primer Zhou and self-assertion as "the representative of the correct path" through the *Fengqing* Incident, for the purpose of seizing power at the Fourth National People's Congress (NPC).[1]

On January 26, 1977, another article published in the *People's Daily*, written by Wang Huide and titled "An Anti-Revolutionary Liar Specializes in Selling Counterfeit Drugs," criticized Zhang Chunqiao's "On All-Round Dictatorship over the Capitalist Class" from April 1975, revealing his conspiracy of distorting Marxism in the name of Marxism. Likewise, a contributing commentator of *Red Flag* wrote in the 10th issue of the magazine in 1978 the article "Proletarian Dictatorship and Socialist Democracy," mounting a full-scale political and theoretical attack against Zhang's "all-round dictatorship," which embodied the Gang's conspiracy in overthrowing Party rule, implementing Fascist rule, and shattering proletarian rule.

The same issue of *Red Flag* featured a long editorial titled "On Yao Wenyuan," which debunked his confounding of the truth by manipulating public opinion in favor of the Gang.

Criticism was also directed against the Gang's own campaign writing teams, which were manipulated as the "canons" for fueling anti-revolutionary opinion. At the forefront of the anti-revolutionary battlefield were the Mass Criticism Group of the Peking and Tsinghua Universities, which took the collective penname of Liang Xiao 梁效 (the homophone of "two colleges"), and the writing group of the Shanghai Municipal Party Committee, which went by the pseudonym of Luo Siding 羅思鼎. The former was placed under the leadership of Jiang Qing, while the latter acted under the direct command of Yao Wenyuan and Zhang Chunqiao. Other examples of the Gang's writing teams included what were known as Chi Heng 池恒, groomed by Yao and attached to the *Red Flag* editorial board, as well as Tang Xiaowen 唐曉文 and Chu Lan 初瀾, under the helm of Jiang. In retrospect, the *People's Daily* published two detailed critiques of Liang Xiao's essence as the Gang's most honored mouthpiece and baton of reactionary activities. The first of these, titled "An Anti-Revolutionary Task Force of the Gang of Four," was contributed by a Xinhua reporter and correspondent and issued on July 13, 1977, whereas the other, "On Liang Xiao" by the CPC Peking University Committee, was released on March 21, 1978. Regarding Luo Siding, the *People's Daily* had "On Luo Siding" by Shen Taosheng on August 15, 1977. The article recorded the group's publication of its first reactionary article in November 1973, where Premier Zhou was implicitly compared to chancellors of imperial China, as well as its practice of "admiring the Legalists" for the sake of ascending the Gang of Four to power.[2] In "On Chi Heng" in its eighth issue in 1978, *Red Flag*, too, condemned Yao's control of the Chi Heng writing group with a focus on his fabrication about the existence of a bourgeois class in the Party. On December 15, 1977, Shen Tao followed up the waves of criticism by another article targeted at Jiang Qing's Chu Lan under the title "Raging Waves of Conspiracy against Art and Literature," also published in the *People's Daily*.

Another political weapon of their reactionary agenda, the so-called "revolutionary newspapers" and other publications patronized by Lin and the Gang became another major target of rectification for post-Cultural Revolution journalism. On March 17, 1977, "Digging One's Own Graves and Building One's Own Grave Stones" by a Xinhua reporter and correspondent was released through *Guangming Daily*, exposing the manipulative nature of *Study and Criticism* (*Xüexi yu pipan* 學習與批判). On May 29, 1978, *Zhejiang Daily* (*Zhejiang ribao* 浙江日報) published the Mass Criticism Group of the Zhejiang Federation of Trade Unions' "A Localized Anti-Revolutionary Gang Paper" targeted at the *Zhejiang Workers' Daily* (*Zhejiang gongren ribao* 浙江工人日報), which was usurped by the Gang's subordinates in the province. Moreover, in "Conspiracy between the Gang and Lin via the Lens of *The Workers' Revolt* (*Gongren zuofan bu* 工人造反報)" in Shanghai's *Liberation Daily*, Chen Tao argued that the Gang's direct control of the paper was evidence of their conspiracy with Lin Biao.

The denunciation of the publicity of misleading role models

With the progression of the mass campaign to criticize Lin and the Gang, the print media began to expose misleading role models they were forced to publicize under the control of the Gang and to invite the masses to join their denunciation. It was the *People's Daily* that pioneered such a tide of criticism, starting with its publication of a letter written by a worker of the Shanghai Fifth Steel Plant alongside an editors' note. The letter noted that between 1974 and October 1976, the *People's Daily* published a total of 60 stories publicizing the Plant's alleged experience in appreciating the Legalists and criticizing the Confucians as well as practicing the "only productivity theory," while the editors' note made the further comment that the Plant was set up as a prototype in order to negate the traditional Daqing model. The editors' note continued to stand by Mao while condemning the Gang: "The whole Party running a newspaper was a direction of newspaper-running designated by Chairman Mao. We hope our readers will expose all crimes we committed under the control of the Gang of Four, so that all poisonous influence can be eliminated."

On November 30, 1976, the *People's Daily* released an investigation report titled "An Anti-revolutionary Political Fraud," unraveling the Gang and Mao Yuanxin's publicity of the unseemly "blank answer sheet hero" Zhang Tiesheng.[3]

On November 26, 1977, the paper featured an older investigation report directed against Zhang, which was produced during the Cultural Revolution by a young intellectual named Dong Jinshuo who decided to return to his native place, with the title "Just Adjudication Has Finally Arrived!", alongside an editors' note.

The *Beijing Daily* (*Beijing ribao* 北京日報) followed suit. After publishing its own mass criticism group's "The First Step of the Gang of Four's Power Usurpation" on April 24, 1978, it put out Zhu Nanshu's "Uncovering the Truth of 'A Letter and Diary Abstracts from A Primary School Student'" against Chi Qun and Xie Jingyi's reporting of the undesirable young prototype.[4] The *People's Daily* also conducted an investigation of the same incident and published the results in the report "Exposing a Political Fraud: The Truth of 'A Letter and Diary Abstracts from A Primary School Student'" on May 21, 1978.

Another news story denounced by the *People's Daily* concerned the promotion of experience of the Chaoyang Agricultural University, which the Gang lauded as a determined effort against the practice of the past 17 years, as published in "An Anti-Revolutionary Experience of Power Usurpation" on February 21, 1978.[5]

Finally, there was "Exterminating the Pernicious Influences of the Ha'ertao Experience," an article written by the Liaoling Provincial Association of Supply and Marketing Cooperatives and published also by the *People's Daily*, in condemnation of the Gang and Mao Yuanxin's promotion of the Ha'ertao model, which dealt a heavy blow to the rural economy.[6]

The denunciation of the inducement of injustices through the print media

Also widely published were articles denouncing Lin and the Gang's inducement of injustices making use of the print media.

In 1978, the *People's Daily* featured two articles with the title "The Truth of the Tiananmen Incident" consecutively on November 21 and 22, criticizing the Gang's false incrimination of Deng Xiaoping and the masses. Similarly, *Red Flag*'s "An Encirclement of the Anti-revolutionary by Public Opinion" in its 12th issue in 1978 condemned the Gang's manipulation of the magazine in suppressing the April Fifth Movement in Tiananmen Square.

On December 29, 1978, the Shanghai *Liberation Daily* and *Wenhui Bao* both published Gao Zhi's "A Big Case of Injustice that Strikes the Nation," debunking the notorious article that started off the Cultural Revolution and led to the false accusation of Wu Han, "On the New Historical Play *Dismissal of Hai Rui*." On February 22, 1979, Li Yan's "A Flare Declaring the Launch of Anti-Revolutionary Power Seizure" was featured in the *People's Liberation Army Daily*. On top of the article's criticism of the newspaper's publication of "To Attack the Anti-Party and Anti-Socialism Reactionary Force," which was signed 高炬 but in fact written under the instruction of Jiang Qing, the appended editors' note added that articles published with this pseudonym had brought tremendous injustice to the columns of satirical essays "Evening Talks at Yanshan" (*Yanshan yehua* 燕山夜話) and "Notes from Three-Family Village" (*Sanjia cun zhaji* 三家村劄記), their authors, and their publishers, namely, *The Battlefront* (*Qianxian* 前線) magazine, *Beijing Evening News* (*Beijing wanbao* 北京晚報), and *Beijing Daily*. Similar articles of rectification were also found in the *Beijing Daily*, the *People's Daily*, and Xinhua releases during the period.

Moreover, the *People's Daily* published a series of articles on June 30, July 7, and July 16, 1977 to criticize the forced publication of the editorial "Grasp the Crucial Points and Criticize Deng in Depth" on August 23, 1976, and vindicate such documents as Deng's *On the General Program of Work for the Whole Party and the Whole Nation* (*Lun quandang quanguo gexiang gongzuo de zonggang* 論全黨全國各項工作的總綱), *Some Questions Concerning the Acceleration of Industrial Development* (*Guanyu jiakuai gongye fazhan de ruogan wenti* 關於加快工業發展的若干問題), and Hu Yaobang's *Several Questions Concerning Work on Science and Technology: Outline of the Works Report of the Chinese Academy of Sciences* (*Guanyu keji gongzhou de jige wenti — zhongguo kexue yuan gongzuo huibao tigang* 關於科技工作的幾個問題——中國科學院工作彙報提綱).

On December 24 of the same year, the *People's Daily* published "Uncovering the Unjust Case of Wang Yazhuo," jointly written by Wang Wenyao, En Yali, and Xing Zhuo, with an appended editors' note that the Wang Yazhuo case was but an example of the paper's false accusations when it was at the beck and call of the Gang.[7]

The denunciation of the anti-revolutionary journalism theory and the "Gang eight-legged style"

By forcing their version of journalism theory and copious style of writing resembling the ancient eight-legged essays upon the news media, Lin and the Gang had shaken the tradition of journalism, which the industry was eager to restore after their fall. Hence, such journalism theory and the "Gang eight-legged style" (*bang bagu* 幫八股) also became an important area of critique.

To begin with, Xu Zhankun's "Condemning the Theory of Facts Submitting to the Needs of the Line," published in the *People's Daily* on March 26, 1978, criticized that the Gang not only had the means, but also a theory of spreading rumors. It revealed the fallacious hidden meaning of this theory as deception through selective reporting, contending that the distortion of facts would only cost the trust of the people and the Party's reputation in the long run.

Both "Resolutely Tear Down the Gang of Four's Theory of the Blank Line Dictatorship of Journalism" in *Nanfang Daily* (*Nanfang ribao* 南方日報) on April 21, 1978 and "Revolution and Anti-Revolution at the Battlefront" in the first issue of *The Press* (*Xinwen zhanxian* 新聞戰線) in 1978 denounced the article "To Thoroughly Implement the Great Revolution on the News Line," a work of Chen Boda and Yao Wenyuan, as the "theoretical foundation" backing the anti-revolutionary groups' manipulation of the print media.

Ren Ping's "Crushing the Gang Eight-Legged Style," and the short commentary "To be Frank," both appearing in the *People's Daily* on February 21, 1977, made sharp attacks on the Gang's pompous style of speech and writing, as compared to the redundant eight-legged essays. The former argued that under the influence of the Gang, literary style went beyond the scope of language and writing skills, but was subjugated by political ideology, whereas the latter advocated the integrity of journalists amid criticism.

On October 18,1977, December 24,1977, and October 14,1978, the *People's Liberation Army Daily* published three editors' commentaries by the title of "Literary Rectification Beginning with the Word 'False,'" which provided a comprehensive review of the emergence and development of falsified news stories and gave suggestions on corresponding remedies. On November 13, 1977, an article by the paper's commentator "Eliminate All Empty Talk" equated empty talk with lies, citing examples from top-down instructions, bottom-up reports, speeches, meetings, and news stories. During the post-cultural revolution years, it took the journalists tremendous effort to rectify the once celebrated style of empty, bogus speech and writing.

Discussions on "Practice is the Sole Criterion for Testing Truth"

The real turning point did not arrive until two years after the smashing of the Gang of Four, or the convention of the Third Plenary Session of the 11th CPC Central Committee. Before that, Party leader Hua Guofeng had insisted on the principle of the Two Whatevers, which proved to be delaying the progress of the rectification of wrongs and the restoration of the right. In May 1978, discussions on the theory "practice is the sole criterion for testing truth" began to take root in newspapers and magazines, breaking the barrier raised up by the Two Whatevers policy, which laid a foundation for the CPC Central Committee meeting held at the end of the year.

The Two Whatevers: a major obstacle to the righting of wrongs

The most pressing tasks for China after the ousting of the Gang of Four included the eradication of the Gang's hierarchical and ideological legacies, the rectification of injustices, including the Tiananmen Incident, the rehabilitation of prestigious and experienced senior cadres such as Deng Xiaoping, and the restoration of the national economy, Socialist democracy, and Socialist legal system against the influence of ultra-leftism. Nonetheless, such quests for righting wrongs were repressed by the then leader Hua Guofeng, who, by perpetuating the worshipping of Mao, sanctioned and promoted the personality cult of himself. His ideology was embodied by his Two Whatevers policy, which summed up a statement made at a Party conference: "We will resolutely uphold whatever policy decisions Chairman Mao made, and unswervingly follow whatever instructions Chairman Mao gave." Upholding Chairman Mao's banner, Hua insisted that the Tiananmen Incident was anti-revolutionary.

As a result, rectification in the news media was confined within the boundary of attacking Lin and the Gang's fabrication of facts as well as the "Gang eight-legged style." Radical revaluation of journalism at the theoretical level was not achieved. Mao's decisions and instructions remained irrefutable, and the glorification of the late chairman, along with his successor, continued. Reports that attempted to challenge the Two Whatevers faced repression and condemnation. For example, the *People's Daily* was prohibited from publishing editorials to commemorate the anniversary of Zhou Enlai's death; the statement that "Comrade Zhou is a great Marxist," too, was banned on account that it did not exist in the Party's official funeral oration for Zhou, which Mao had twice reviewed.

On February 7, 1977, newspapers and magazines throughout the country all published an editorial jointly contributed by the *People's Daily*, *Red Flag*, and the *People's Liberation Army Daily*, titled "Study the Documents Well and Grasp the Key Link," which quoted Hua's declaration: "We will resolutely uphold whatever policy decisions Chairman Mao made, and unswervingly follow whatever instructions Chairman Mao gave." This implied the central sanctioning of continuous class struggle against the "capitalist roaders," and hence the delay of fundamental rectification and rehabilitation.

Struggles preceding the publication of the article "Practice is the Sole Criterion for Testing Truth"

The promulgation of the Two Whatevers amounted to restrictions in the publication of rectification articles. The propaganda authorities prohibited the *People's Daily*'s publication of Zhu De and Chen Yi's poetry and the Tiananmen poems (*Tiananmen shichao* 天安門詩抄), withheld the first issue of the resumed *China Youth* (*Zhongguo qingnian* 中國青年) magazine, which featured the Tiananmen poems and introduced heroes of the April Fifth Movement, and placed a ban on criticism against Zhang Chunqiao's "all-round dictatorship" theory and the faction of the Gang of Four.

This led to strong protests both within the Party and among the masses. Senior cadres such as Deng Xiaoping, Chen Yun, Ye Jianying, and Li Xiannian all expressed vehement opposition against the Two Whatevers. In contention, Deng wrote in a letter to the CPC Central Committee on April 10, 1977, "We must guide the entire Party, the entire military, and all people in the country with accurate and complete Mao Zedong Thought from generation to generation, advancing the undertakings of the Party, Socialism, and international communism in a victorious manner."[8] On May 24, 1977, Deng made an explicit criticism against Hua's insistence on the Two Whatevers in the March Central Work Conference. In July 1977, Deng was restored to all his former posts in the Party and the government at the Third Plenary Session of the 11th CPC Central Committee, where he enunciated the need of a comprehensive and accurate understanding of Mao Zedong Thought instead of reading it from sporadic phrases, lest it should be distorted.

Following this, the news media began to publish articles aiming at righting wrongs on both theoretical and policy bases, under the patronage of the older-generation Party leaders.

The thorough criticism of Lin and Jiang's forging of "black line dictatorship" started at the *People's Daily* with the support of Deng. On August 8, 1977, Deng pointed out in a science and education seminar that it had been the "red line" that dominated national education throughout the past 17 years since the founding of the PRC, and most of the nation's intellectuals served socialism voluntarily. Soon, in September, a *People's Daily* reporter wrote an account of the course of the Gang's compilation of the *Summary of the National Conference on Education Work* (*Quanguo jiaoyu gongzuo huiyi jiyao* 全國教育工作會議紀要), and submitted it to the Party leadership. On November 18, 1977, the paper published an article titled "How were the 'Two Appraisals' Forged?" against the Gang's accusations that, first, education was usurped by the capitalists from the hands of the proletarians, tantamount to a "black line dictatorship," and second, most intellectuals belonged to the capitalist class. On November 20, the *People's Daily* held a seminar for the artists and literati, investigating into and refuting the "black line dictatorship" accusation in the fields of publication, physical education, public health, and public security.

Improvements were also found in news propaganda under Deng's leadership. From February 1978 onwards, the Central People's Broadcasting Station stopped broadcasting the program *Quotations from Chairman Mao* (*Mao zhuxi yulu* 毛主席語錄). Another precedent was set on March 22, 1978, when the *People's Daily* stopped bolding Deng's quotation of Mao's words in its publication of Deng's "Speech at the Opening Ceremony of the National Conference on Science," as the reformist leader requested. From then on, quotations of the Party's revolutionary leaders were no longer highlighted in bold. Moreover, quotations were taken down from the column next to the newspaper masthead and significantly reduced in the text; gigantic photographs of Party leaders were excluded; titles of leaders were changed, as were the arrangement of news on leaders' public activities. The most impressive was Deng's admission of China's relative economic and technological backwardness compared with capitalist countries at the National Science Conference, which shed light on the reform of the news media in the near future.

The publication of "Practice is the Sole Criterion for Testing Truth" and the discussions on truth

The 11th National Congress of the CPC convened in August 1977 failed to correct the theories, policies, and slogans of the Cultural Revolution, but rather, reinforced them. With the ongoing progress of rectification, two questions became increasingly topical: Should China follow the Two Whatevers principle or abide by the pragmatic approach of "seeking truth from facts" (實是求是 *shishi qiushi*)? What constitutes the truth?

In fact, before that, *Guangming Daily* had received a theoretical essay from Nanjing University Professor of Philosophy Hu Fuming, namely, "Practice is a Criterion for Testing Truth." Soon accepted by the editorial team, its publication was only delayed due to amendments based on correspondence between the editors and the author.

The amendments were made to sharpen the argument. This was accredited to Yang Xiguang, who was assigned a leadership position at *Guangming Daily* in March 1978 while receiving education in the Party School of the Central Committee of the CPC. Seeing great value in Hu's article, he decided to remove it from the paper's philosophy section and place it at a more important position on the front page after fine-tuning.

Substantial modifications were made with the joint effort of the author and the editorial team. The article was then sent to the Theory Research Center of the Party School of the Central Committee of the CPC for further refinement before being finalized by Hu Yaobang, who was then the School's vice president. It was eventually released on May 10, 1978, first in the CPC Central Committee's internal publication *Theoretical Trends* (*Lilun dongtai* 理論動態) under the title "Practice is the Sole Criterion for Testing Truth" (with an acknowledgement of *Guangming Daily* as the source).

A day later, the article came out in *Guangming Daily*, signed the newspaper's "Contributing Commentator." It was simultaneously released by Xinhua throughout the country, resulting in its appearance in the *People's Daily*, the *People's Liberation Army Daily*, and seven provincial-level newspapers on the next day. Until the end of May, a total of 30 newspapers in China had reprinted the article.

"Practice is the Sole Criterion for Testing Truth" explicates the major Marxist principles concerning the criterion of truth. Arguing that tests of truth "cannot be found in subjective areas," and "thoughts and theories cannot be tests of their own objectivity and practicality," it suggests that "only through the social practice of thousands and thousands of people can the mission of testing truth be accomplished." It also makes a poignant challenge to the Two Whatevers, commenting that one must have the courage to touch the "forbidden zones" of thoughts set up by the Gang of Four and to "clarify what is right and wrong."

The article turned out to be the most thought-provoking of its kind since the onset of rectification. Its publication aroused two contradictory responses. While it received accolades from numerous Party cadres and the majority of the masses, attacks from followers of the Two Whatevers were fierce. The propaganda authorities criticized that it was "spearheaded against Chairman Mao" and the newspaper that published it "had no Party spirit," to the state of questioning "which central committee the opinions came from." In a nutshell, the article marked the beginning of a hot debate concerning the criterion of truth.

The older-generation proletarian revolutionaries represented by Deng Xiaoping, Li Xiannian, Tan Zhenlin, Luo Ruixing, and Hu Yaobang showed open approval for the Marxist views expressed in the article and the discussion of truth. Against pressure from the supporters of the Two Whatevers, Deng made an impressive statement at the All-Army Conference on Political Work:

> There are other comrades, however, who talk about Mao Zedong Thought every day, but who often forget, abandon, or even oppose Comrade Mao's fundamental Marxist viewpoint and his method of seeking truth from facts, of always proceeding from reality and of integrating theory with practice. Some people even go further: they maintain that those who persist in seeking truth from facts, proceeding from reality and integrating

theory with practice are guilty of a heinous crime. In essence, their view is that one need only parrot what was said by Marx, Lenin and Comrade Mao Zedong — that it is enough to reproduce their words mechanically. According to them, to do otherwise is to go against Marxism-Leninism and Mao Zedong Thought and against the guidelines of the Central Committee. This issue they have raised is no minor one, for it involves our general approach to Marxism-Leninism and Mao Zedong Thought ... We must eliminate the poisonous influence of Lin Biao and the Gang of Four, set things right, and cast off our mental shackles so that we can really emancipate our minds.[9]

On June 6, this speech was published by the *People's Daily* in a prominent position with a catchy headline on the front page. It became a pillar of support for journalists and those engaged in the study of theories in the matter of the criterion of truth.

On June 24, the *People's Liberation Army Daily* published an article under the anonymous name of the paper's "contributing commentator," titled "The Most Fundamental Principle of Marxism." Retorting criticisms against "Practice is the Sole Criterion for Testing Truth" from a theoretical point of view, it was written by a Party member studying at the Party School and modified by Military Commission Secretary-General Luo Ruiqing. Despite political risk, it was later distributed by Xinhua, and then reprinted in newspapers like the *People's Daily* and *Guangming Daily*.

Between June and December 1978, Deng made numerous speeches affirming the significance of discussing the criterion of truth and criticizing the Two Whatevers. On September 16, he said during a visit to the Northeast:

As you all know, there is a doctrine known as the Two Whatevers. Hasn't it become famous? According to this doctrine, whatever documents Comrade Mao Zedong read and endorsed and whatever he did and said must always determine our actions, without the slightest deviation. Can this be called holding high the banner of Mao Zedong Thought? Certainly not! If this goes on, it will debase Mao Zedong Thought.[10]

On December 13, he stressed in a keynote speech at the closing ceremony of the Work Conference of the Central Committee: "Our drive for the Four Modernizations will get nowhere unless rigid thinking is broken down and the minds of cadres and of the masses are completely emancipated."[11] He equated the discussion of the criterion of truth to a debate over the emancipation of the mind, which would be fundamental to the Party and the nation's future.

The discussion was enriched by the enthusiasm of the news media. On October 7, 1978, *China Youth Daily* (*Zhongguo qingnian bao* 中國青年報) printed an excerpt of the third section of Zhou Enlai's report of the first session of the National Youth Congress upon resuming publication. Zhou's argument centered on the demystification of Mao, stating that the late leader should not be promoted as an occasional, born, mysterious, and inimitable leader, which would essentially elevate him into an "isolated god." After being released by Xinhua, it was reprinted by the *People's Daily* and various provincial-level newspapers.

This was followed by reports of speeches and articles by leaders of most provincial administrative divisions and military regions, which all supported the point of view that practice was the sole criterion for testing truth. The challenge to the Two Whatevers eventually led to calls for the rectification of unjust cases, especially the 1976 Tiananmen Incident. The *Workers' Daily* (*Gongren ribao* 工人日報) and *Wenhui Bao*, for example, published some of the Tiananmen poems and the full script of Zong Fuxian's *Where Silence Prevails* (*Yu wu sheng chu* 於無聲處), a stage play written and performed by workers in glorification of the April Fifth Movement. On November 15, 1978, Xinhua reported a groundbreaking announcement by the Beijing Municipal Committee of the CPC, which recognized the 1976 incident as a "revolutionary movement" and declared the rehabilitation of all those persecuted for commemorating Premier Zhou and opposing the Gang of Four. The news was quickly disseminated by the *People's Daily* alongside other local newspapers with large and conspicuous headlines.

One thing noteworthy was that *Red Flag*, the theory magazine of the CPC Central Committee, had stayed away from the debate on the criterion of truth and the Two Whatevers. It only broke its silence in September 1979, when it published the article "Taking Serious Remedial Class for the Discussion of Truth" in its ninth issue.

The momentous Third Plenary Session of the 11th CPC Central Committee was convened from December 18 to 22, 1978. The controversial discussion on the statement "practice is the sole criterion for testing truth" was given high acclaim, which marked a big step forward towards the elimination of ultra-leftism and the emancipation of the mind. Amid this, the contribution of the news media must be acknowledged. In another way round, the debate had the effect of enhancing the image of journalism among the masses as well as journalists' understanding of Marxist theory. Hence, it was as important to the history of journalism as to the history of New China.

Achievements and Failures in Party Journalism after the Third Plenary Session of the 11th CPC Central Committee

The first decade after the Third Plenary Session of the 11th CPC Central Committee saw the conflicting development of the rectification of wrongs and bourgeois liberalism in China's journalism. On the one hand, the news media contributed greatly to the promotion of policy directions adopted since the meeting, including the shift of the focus to economic development, the adherence to the Four Cardinal Principles, the persistence of Reform and Opening Up, and the advancement of Socialist modernization; on the other hand, hostile public opinion such as that instigated between the spring and summer of 1989 brought as much ideological shocks among the masses as it did havoc to the CPC.

The role of journalism in promoting socialist modernization

At the historical watershed following the Third Plenary Session of the 11th CPC Central Committee, the Propaganda Department of the CPC held a National Journalism Seminar from March 8 to 21, 1979. The agenda revolved around two items: the emancipation of the mind at the conclusion of past experience, and how the focus of news propaganda was to be shifted to Socialist economic modernization. In the seminar, Hu Yaobang explicated the nature of Party journalism, the mission of journalism in the New Era, the emancipation of the mind, and the synergy of the merits of motivated, innovative journalists and centralized Party leadership, among other major issues. The twin roles of all types of news media in promoting the CPC's directions, principles, and policies, and in reflecting people's opinions were affirmed.

The in-depth rectification of leftism

Since the spring of 1979, the righting of wrongs and the rehabilitation of unjust cases became China's primary focuses at all fronts. Among all the responsibilities placed on journalism, it was the emancipation of the mind, prompted by the discussions on the criterion of truth and regarded as the prerequisite for rectification, which was first fulfilled.

One major objective of emancipating the mind was to put right what had been reversed by Lin Biao and the Gang of Four so as to free people from the shackles of leftist thought. An even higher mission was the study of new issues and problems facing Socialist modernization and reforms using fundamental Marxist principles. Influential articles in newspapers included Jin Wen's "Is Class Struggle an All-Time Key Link?" published in *Guangming Daily* on January 13, 1979, the first open denial of the slogan "taking class struggle as the key link" in a newspaper. On January 23, Jin made the unprecedented suggestion in "A Thorough Criticism of Lin Biao and the Gang of Four's Malicious Left-Leaning Line" in the same newspaper that the "line" of the anti-revolutionary groups was leftist instead of rightist; the claim that it was superficially leftist but essentially rightist was erroneous. Towards the end of the year, on December 25, 1979, *Guangming Daily* featured one more groundbreaking article by Liu Jiang, titled "Socialism is in Practice" against the hardline belief that Socialism existed only in one form. These articles were reprinted in many other newspapers, casting a huge impact on society.

Journalism played a key role in propagating theories developed during the Party's relearning of Socialism, providing the masses with an outline of the new ideology of Socialism with Chinese characteristics, which covered the following aspects:

- The emancipation of the mind, i.e., to "seek truth from facts" and to regard practice as the sole criterion for testing truth;
- Taking a pathway suited to the national situation in the building of Socialism;
- The necessity of a long initial phase for the building of Socialism under the constraint of economic and cultural backwardness;
- The increase of productivity through modernization;
- The Socialist economy as a planned commodity economy;
- Reform as the major motivation of social development;
- The significance of Socialist democracy and civilization, in conjunction with the Four Cardinal Principles;
- The policy of "One Country, Two System" as a means to reunification;
- The vital importance of the conduct of the ruling Party;
- The establishment of relationships with communist parties outside China and other political parties in China according to the principles of autonomy, complete fairness, mutual respect, and mutual non-intervention; and
- Peaceful development as a major subject of the contemporary world.

The most important achievement in the rectification of wrongs was the new insight gained into the long-accepted view of the newspaper as a tool of class struggle based on the denial of "taking class struggle as the key link." Despite the diversity of opinions, an important consensus was reached: the deprived class was gone as far back as in the period of Socialist construction, and class struggle was no longer the major cause of social contradiction; describing the newspaper as a tool of class struggle would be more harmful than meaningful.

Another significant achievement was the reinstatement of Liu Shaoqi's journalism ideology, as established in a series of discussions such as his "Speech to Journalists from North China," which were distorted to slander Liu during the Cultural Revolution. A month after Liu was rehabilitated at the Fifth Plenary Session of the 11th CPC Central Committee in February 1980, the Beijing Journalism Studies Society held a seminar on his journalism ideology. Once again, the entire industry resumed studying and acknowledged Liu's theory of journalism, to the benefit of the emancipation of the mind in the circle.

The waves of rectification of injustices after the Third Plenary Session of the 11th CPC Central Committee were backed by timely news coverage. Articles commemorating deceased older-generation proletarian revolutionaries who had been slandered, persecuted, or purged during the Cultural Revolution, such as Liu Shaoqi, Peng Dehuai, and Tao Zhu flooded newspapers and magazines, with simultaneous exposure of the crimes of Lin and the Gang. At the same time, the news media also reported and publicized centrally-instructed redress efforts of various regions, sectors, and work units. Very often, reports and propaganda of injustices rectified were fused with glorification of dissident heroes who had struggled with the anti-revolutionary groups.

Among these heroes was Zhang Zhixin, a member of the CPC and its Liaoning Propaganda Department. During the Cultural Revolution, she openly expressed her suspicion, dissatisfaction, and indignation towards Lin and the Gang, and refused to compromise even after her arrest in September 1969. As a result, she suffered a slow and painful death from life imprisonment, enduring extreme physical and mental tortures before being decapitated on April 4, 1975.

In early April 1979, the CPC Liaoning Provincial Committee finally held a posthumous rehabilitation conference for Zhang, where she was recognized as a revolutionary martyr. The news first hit the front page of the *Liaoning Daily* (*Liaoning ribao* 遼寧日報) on April 5, followed by *CPC Members'* (*Gongchandang yuan* 共產黨員) feature on the life of Zhang. From April 5 to September, the *Liaoning Daily* spent a total of 28 pages publicizing Zhang's life stories and events that promoted her as a role model. On May 25, 1979, the *People's Daily* published a front page story on Zhang with the headline "Must Struggle for the Truth," which was immediately distributed by Xinhua and then reprinted in many regional newspapers. *Guangming Daily*, *Workers' Daily*, and *China Youth Daily*, among others, all devoted large sections to the heroine's brave deeds. Such stories drew an overwhelming response from the masses. The *People's Daily* alone received over 500 letters from readers throughout the country, praising Zhang's resolute martyrdom and urging the authorities to investigate the legal responsibilities of the chief instigator and executioner of her death.

The publicity of Zhang exemplified a successful propaganda of role models that stirred up an enthusiastic response among the masses. With the onset of the rectification of injustices across the country, progress was also seen in the rehabilitation of the journalism industry itself. On top of redressing injustices, the news media also sought to "seek truth from facts" out of historical issues brought down from the Cultural Revolution.

The news media could by no means escape the injustices imposed by Lin and the Gang of Four. It had been attacked as an "independent anti-revolutionary realm," with all newspapers being "old newspapers that give out poison and spread rumors," and all journalists untrustworthy old personnel. According to Lin and the Gang, cadres at the *People's Daily* had "an evil aura," Xinhua employees were "a basket of rotten tomatoes," and those working for *Red Flag* deserved being "swept away with an iron broom." In general, writing teams of newspapers and magazines were "traitors," "secret agents," "scoundrels and ruffians," "monsters and demons," "remnants of the feudal class," and "bourgeois scholars and authorities." Shortly after the convention of the Third Plenary Session of the 11th CPC Central Committee, Hu Yaobang clarified in his announcement of the Central Committee's resolution to clear the Propaganda Department of the CPC of the accusation of being the Palace of Hell (*Yanwang dian* 閻王殿) that the "battle line" of national propaganda, which included journalism, had always been "revolutionary" rather than "black." The rectification of injustices done to the news media was embarked upon.

The accusation of the Three-Family Village as an anti-party gang was the first major injustice done to the news media during the Cultural Revolution. In early 1979, the *Beijing Daily*, *People's Liberation Army Daily*, and *People's Daily* successively published articles seeking redress for the case. On January 26, the *Beijing Daily* published an article written by some of the editors of *Red Flag*, titled "A Striking Anti-Revolutionary Seditious Incident: the Three-Family Village Unjust Case." The *People's Liberation Army Daily*, as mentioned earlier, printed Li Yan's "A Flare Declaring the Launch of Anti-Revolutionary Power Seizure: Criticism of Gao Ju's 'To Attack the Anti-Party and Anti-Socialism Reactionary Force'" on February 22 with an editors' note. The *People's Daily* featured Ren Wenping's "A Startling Literary Inquisition: Rehabilitation of 'Notes from Three-Family Village' and

'Evening Talks at Yanshan,'" also with an editors' note, on the same day. Eventually, media efforts found official sanction in the CPC Central Committee's approval of the full rehabilitation of the unjustly-accused Deng Ta, Wu Han, and Liao Mosha.

Another deep blow to the journalism field during the Cultural Revolution was a literary inquisition that condemned the satirical column "A Record of Strengths and Weaknesses" (*Changduan lu* 長短錄) in the *People's Daily*'s supplement alongside "Evening Talks at Yanshan" and "Notes from Three-Family Village" as "big poisonous weeds" against the Party and Socialism. Apart from the writers and editors of these columns, all labeled as "anti-Party elements," columns of many other newspapers were also identified as "branch stores" of the so-called Three-Family Village and "anti-revolutionary tools" of "A Record of Strengths and Weaknesses." Not only were their writers and editors implicated; even readers who had shown appreciation to these essays were afflicted. Thus, after the rectification of the Three-Family Village case, the case of "A Record of Strengths and Weaknesses" was put right; and hence the rehabilitation of writers Xia Yan, Wu Han, Liao Mosha, Meng Chao, and Tang Tao, together with the column's person-in-charge Chen Xiaoyu, among whom Wu, Meng, and Chen had been persecuted to death.

Many other journalists died unjust deaths during the Cultural Revolution. Following the suicide of the intellectual Deng Tuo, renowned journalist Fan Changjiang followed in his footsteps suffering immense torment. The news media started redressing Fan in the spring of 1979. To commemorate him and his works, *The Press* republished his articles "Random Thoughts of a Journalist's Work" in its first issue in 1979. In this period, a lot of famous journalists persecuted by Lin, the Gang, and Kang Sheng were redressed, many of them posthumously. Apart from Pan Zinian, Zhang Hanfu, Mengqiu Jiang, Jin Zhonghua, and Gao Lisheng, who did not live through the Cultural Revolution, the big names included Chen Kehan, who became disabled, and Yun Yiqun, who withstood prolonged persecution.

Even the deceased journalist, political critic, and publisher Zou Taofen had been defamed as a "black-liner" and "black shop owner" of the 1930s, his former residence being shut down. To restore the name of the celebrated personality, *The Press* published Mao Zedong and Zhou Enlai's inscriptions in commemoration of Zou's death in its third issue in 1979.

The spring of 1979 was also the time when Fudan University redressed its wrong judgment of Professor of Journalism Wang Zhong, who was rendered a rightist for a speech in 1957.

To China's journalism, the waves of redress and rehabilitation following the Cultural Revolution constituted a new round of Marxist education. The period not only bred the political situation necessary for the stability and coherence of the industry; it also created a favorable academic environment for journalism research.

The key role of economic news propaganda

The shift of the focus of journalism to economic propaganda, initiated by the CPC Propaganda Department, was reflected in the quantity and quality of economic news released after the March 1979 National Journalism Seminar. There was a surge in media coverage of economic news. To take Xinhua as an example, in the year 1984, economic news accounted for 84% of its domestic releases and the majority of its international dispatches. More importantly, economic news had been liberated from the once-pervasive rigid style, emerging beyond sheer discussion of production to penetrate into diverse aspects of economic life, including circulation, distribution, exchange, and consumption. In addition, "seeking truth from facts" and pragmatism became the guiding principles of economic news propaganda, as opposed to subjectivity, authoritarianism, and formalism.

Rural economic reform

Prototypical of such economic propaganda were news reports on the establishment of the agricultural production responsibility system, which epitomized the changes in rural areas following the Third Plenary Session of the 11th CPC Central Committee. The dominant form was the household contract responsibility system that fused centralized and decentralized operations so as to leverage the advantages of both public ownership and household businesses. News propaganda on various forms of the production responsibility system can be analyzed in three stages.

(1) Stage 1: Before and after the Third Plenary Session of the 11th CPC Central Committee

In early 1978, the news media started publicizing the reinstatement of effective policies with rural areas, including the respect for the autonomy of production teams, the restoration of household sideline businesses, and the opening of rural markets, according to Deng's public announcements. Starting from January 1979, the release of the *Decision of the CPC Central Committee on Some Questions Concerning the Acceleration of Agricultural Development (Draft) (Zhonggong zhongyang guanyu jiakuai nongye fazhan ruogan wenti de jueding (cao'an)* 中共中央關於加快農業發展若干問題的決定（草案）) sparked off the promotion of the systems of "contracting tasks to work groups" (*baogong daozu* 包工到組) and "linking output to payments" (*lianchan jichou* 聯產 計酬). As for the spontaneously-emerging "contracting production quotas to households" (*baochan daohu* 包產到戶), it was not yet publicized as the official green light had not yet been given.

At the same time, there was reverse propaganda that puzzled the cadres and masses. An example was a letter to the editor from Luoyang, Henan, published on the front page of the *People's Daily* on March 15, which criticized "linking output to work groups" (*lianchan daozu* 聯產到組) as a step backward from the three-tier ownership system that held the production team as the foundation (*sanji suoyou, dui wei jichu* 三級所有，隊為基礎). Realizing the confusion it brought, the paper remedied the situation by publishing letters that held an opposite opinion. Articles that accomplished the propaganda purpose included *Liaoning Daily* reporter Fan Jingyi's "Distinguish between the Mainstream and Tributaries, Do Not Mistake the Beginning as Overdoing," where he made an analysis of the situation of rural Liaoning. The article was reprinted in the *People's Daily* on May 16, 1979 with an editors' note in approval of Fan's attitude and point of view: "As journalists, we should follow Fan Jingyi's example in conducting solid surveys, answering comrades who hold suspicions or disagreements about the spirit of the Third Plenary Session with facts."

(2) Before and after the dispatch of the *Notice on Several Questions Concerning the Further Reinforcement and Perfection of the Agricultural Production Responsibility System* (*Guanyu jinyibu jiaqiang he wanshan nongye shengchan zeren zhi de ji ge wenti* 關於進一步加強和完善農業生產責任制的幾 個問題) in September 1980.

As mentioned, the system of "contracting production quotas to households" had been in force in some rural areas, such as Anhui. On August 8, 1979, *Anhui Daily* reported the practice of *Dabaogan* 大包幹 (full contract responsibility system) in rural Fengyang. Later, in April 1980, the *People's Daily* printed Wu Xiang and Zhang Guangyou's "Output-Based Responsibility Systems Have Many Benefits" which introduced the Anhui experience. Despite the terminology, the concept of individual responsibility over one's output quota (*zeren dao ren* 責任到人) elucidated in the article was essentially an equivalent of "contracting production quotas to households." This made the article controversial, as the September 1980 notice had granted the system no more than an ad hoc status in remote mountainous regions and places of destitution, for the purpose of meeting subsistence needs. In the period, media support for the systems of "contracting production quotas to households" and

Dabaogan was mainly constrained to indirect promotion through introducing prototypical experiences with the output-based responsibility systems as a whole. Rural cadres and residents felt much encouraged by the *People's Daily*'s move, and they regarded the article as a guarantee and guidance for the implementation of the production responsibility system.

(3) Before and after the adoption of the *Summary of the National Rural Work Conference* (*Quanguo nongcun gongzuo huiyi jiyao* 全國農村工作會議紀要) in January 1982.

The Summary stated that over 90% of the production teams in all rural areas had developed various kinds of production responsibility systems; drastic changes were giving way to a phase of conclusion, completion, and stability. From then on, the news media turned to publicize stable and comprehensive models and report new phenomena and trends in rural areas.

Propaganda of these model systems had three focuses: First, the differentiation between "contracting production quotas to households," or *Dabaogan*, and "leasing land for household farming" (*fantien dangan* 分田單幹). In other words, the production responsibility system shall remain within the Socialist collective economy, suiting China's current national situation and productivity. Second, the introduction of exemplary systems, including the system of economic contracts, carried out in places like Anhui in order to highlight the superiority of "contracting." Third, commentaries regarding questions and problems related to the implementation of the production responsibility system. The message of "unchanged policy" was publicized to stabilize confidence, while practices that threatened collective property were denounced.

Meanwhile, places that pioneered "contracting production quotas to households" and *Dabaogan* soon groomed a host of specialized households and new cooperative groups. Instead of putting out a barrage of experiences, the news media acted with restraint, restricting their coverage to the most typical examples, while at the same time analyzing these new bodies as necessary trends of the production and development of rural commodities. Propaganda was strengthened after the convention of the 12th CPC Central Committee, substantiated with topical discussions.

All in all, news coverage of the advancement of the agricultural production responsibility system and the development of the rural commodity economy after the Third Plenary Session of the 11th CPC Central Committee set a model for economic news propaganda during the New Era. Two important principles were established:

First, the upholding of Marxist epistemology against ultra-leftism. Marxist epistemology was promoted as an anecdote to the adverse influences of ultra-leftism to which rural China had long been subject. As Socialism had been supplanted by egalitarianism and criticized as capitalism, large efforts were directed to expound the true meaning of Socialism as well as to promote the Socialist nature of the production responsibility system and the rural commodity economy. In the face of disguised forms of "leasing land for household farming" or the infringement of collective property, the media ascribed such chaos to transitory inefficient local leadership, dismissing charges against the CPC's rural policy. Likewise, the disintegration of the collective economy in certain places was explained as the side-effect of prolonged ultra-leftism, as opposed to the consequence of a rightist approach.

The second was the upholding of the "mass line," i.e., respecting the innovative spirit, will, and opinion of the masses without engaging in rivalries. Such leftist means as creating opinion pressures and stirring up severe criticisms were replaced with the stability-oriented approaches of initiating discussions and introducing prototypical models. The *People's Daily* was exemplary in this respect. Starting from the beginning of 1979, it brought up the discussion of "How to accelerate agricultural development," devoting 50 issues to the topic over the course of a year. In 1980, it introduced another topic, "How farmers can gain wealth as soon as possible," and in 1981, two more: "How to speed up the circulation of commodities" and "Chen Zhixiong contracting collective fishponds." Usually given in first person by those involved, the opinions thus gathered were more easily accepted by the rural cadres and proved more valuable to the masses.

Urban economic reform

With the initial success of the rural economic reform, the CPC decided to expand its reform efforts to the entire economy, taking urban areas as the focal point. After the Third Plenary Session of the 12th CPC Central Committee on October 20, 1984, urban reform rose to the center stage of economic news propaganda. Although propaganda of the urban reform was more challenging, the media benefited from their prior experience in publicizing its rural counterpart.

While China's economy was much vitalized by the urban-centered economic reform, tension between the new and old systems entailed contradictory responses across society. Moreover, difficulties in work and life, especially after the acceleration of urban reform in October 1984, gave rise to uncertainties and anxiety. This made the news media's role in propagating the ideology, theories, and policies of the economic reform all the more important. It was no coincidence that the decade of China's economic reform yielded the most productive years of economic commentaries. During the period, the *People's Daily*, *Economic Daily* (*Jingji ribao* 經濟日報), *Workers' Daily*, and other newspapers frequently published opinion-shaping articles based on surveys and research. The *People's Daily*, for example, introduced a series of editorials advocating the importance of acting within the nation's capability since April 1979 in order to promote the CPC Central Committee's national economic principles of "adjustment, reform, rectification, and improvement." In 1982, it issued another series of editorials under the title "On the Unfeasibility of Eating *Daguofan*," examining the flaws of the old fixed payment system. From the national Xinhua News Agency and Central People's Broadcasting Station to regional newspapers and radio stations, all sectors of the news media expanded their energy in producing economic commentaries in accord with the pace of reform. The mushrooming of short commentaries was particularly worth noting, as they provided focused, in-depth analyses to single issues of public concern, boosting public confidence in the reform.

Among the media industry, the newspaper showed a clear edge in leading the discussion of theoretical questions regarding the urban economic reform. From November 1979 onwards, the *People's Daily* spent over a month on the "clarification of the production objective of Socialism," which was provoked by a contributing commentator's article on the same topic, published on October 20. Given the far-reaching theoretical and practical significance of the question, compounded with society's general inconsistency in understanding it, the discussion quickly drew the attention and participation of all walks of life across the nation. Eventually, it led to the consensus that the objective of Socialist production was to fulfill people's increasing material and cultural needs, against which the nation would run the risk of toppling the balance of its economy. This was pivotal to the adjustment of the national economic structure, as characterized by the growth of light industries (especially textile), the shrinking of heavy industries, and the integration of civil and military production. In the days that followed, further discussions on the standard of productivity, also spearheaded by the *People's Daily*, developed into the backbone of the theory that China was in the "primary stage of socialism," on top of driving urban economic reform.

Newspaper-led discussions also contributed greatly to the exploration of new phenomena and problems which extended beyond the original policy scope or deviated from the original policy. In June and July 1987, the *Economic Daily* started off a discussion on whether leased enterprises were "Socialist" or "capitalist" by nature, dubbed the "Guan Guangmei phenomenon." Picking up on the controversy over Guan Guangmei's operation of eight leased stores, the discussion not only aroused vehement domestic response, but also caught the eyes of foreign media, for it cut straight to the question of whether operation and ownership rights should be separated, which had already stirred up debate in Benxi two years before. By providing room for the contribution of its editors, reporters, and readers instead of avoiding the controversial crux of the problem or passing quick judgment, the *Economic Daily*'s initiative effectively advanced the development of economic theories and policies.

News stories on prototypical models, some in greater depths than the others, both showed approval to revolutionary and energetic entrepreneurs born out of the economic reform and added impetus to the reform of enterprises and the entire economic system. On the other hand, the news media was as concerned about the failures of certain pioneering enterprise leaders, who were beaten by an unfavorable environment, entangled in an investigation, or dismissed from office. As an example, from April 22 to May 8, 1986, *China Youth Daily* published a news series titled "Revelation from Young Factory Directors' Reform and Exploration," analyzing the subjective and objective as well as institutional and ideological causes of the lapses of young pioneers in some typical cases.

Critical news stories of negative examples or flaws related to economic development were no less stimulating to the urban economic reform. From February 9, 1983, the Central People's Broadcasting Station provided three months of continuous coverage of a barbaric unloading incident at the Shuangchengbao Railway Station, Harbin, releasing 32 pieces of news, commentaries, and audio reports in total.[12] Subsequently, the radio station persisted in following up on the progress of improvements succeeding the change of leadership in the railway station. Such instances of critical journalism were welcomed by government leaders and all sectors of society. The *People's Daily*, *Economic Daily*, *China Youth Daily*, and *People's Railway Daily* joined to bring added pressure to resolve the incident. Later, the *Economic Daily*'s report of the decline of the quality of refrigerators manufactured by Xuehua across three months since August 15, 1986 created another example of how the exposure of negligence in quality could push forward enterprise management reforms.

Plentiful news stories of regional models of urban economic reform were presented in varying angles. Some of these regions were the Shenzhen Special Economic Zone, which gave birth to Chinese-foreign joint ventures and foreign enterprises; Wuxi, Suzhou, and Changzhou of Jiangxu, which bred village and township enterprises; Wenzhou of Zhejiang, which established its fame from cottage industries; and Hainan, the largest pilot zone of the economic reform.

A product of news propaganda for the urban economic reform was "in-depth reporting," such as that about the Lubuge Hydroelectric Project by the *People's Daily* on August 6, 1987.[13] Such in-depth stories were characterized by a departure from the focus on a single person or single event in favor of a broad view on the entire reform, aiming at informing readers with wider perspectives from the underlying background to the trends of future development.

Generally speaking, despite such blemishes as one-sidedness, absoluteness, media hype, and the propagation of inappropriate slogans, economic propaganda in the New Era succeeded in drumming up support for the economic reform. Moreover, when economic overheating was detected, the media managed to contribute to the cooling-down of the economy following the instruction of the CPC. It is perhaps fair to call the decade a "golden age" of economic news propaganda — vibrant, controlled, and effective — in the history of the People's Republic of China.

The building of "Socialist spiritual civilization"

If economic news propaganda played a leading role in the attainment of "material civilization," media contributions in shoring up the building of "spiritual civilization" deserved as much attention.

The concepts of "material civilization" and "spiritual civilization" were advocated by Deng and officially endorsed in the report of the 12th CPC National Congress, passed in September 1982: "While establishing a high degree of material civilization, we must make an effort in building a high degree of Socialist spiritual civilization."[14] In December, the Fifth Planetary Session of the Fifth NPC adopted the *Constitution of the People's Republic of China* (*Zhonghua renmin gongheguo xianfa* 中華人民共和國憲法), which laid down clear provisions regarding the strengthening of the "Socialist spiritual civilization." Finally, the *Decision of the CPC Central Committee on the Guiding Principles of the Construction of Socialist Spiritual Civilization* (*Zhonggong zhongyang guanyu shehui zhuyi jingshen wenming jianshe zhidao fangzhen de jueyi* 中共中央關於社會主義精神文明建設指導方針的決議) adopted in September 1986 gave further details with respect to the strategic position, objective, and guiding principles. These documents provided the guideline for news propaganda on the building of "Socialist spiritual civilization."

The building of "Socialist spiritual civilization" involved the two broad fields of ideological and moral values, and education, science, and culture, the former outlining its nature and general direction. Therefore, the news media placed great emphasis on ideological and moral education, advocating the values of Communism, Socialism, collectivism, patriotism, and serving the people.

Communist values

The propagation of communist values was emphasized due to the emergence of skepticism towards the ideals and morals of Communism after the Cultural Revolution, especially among the youth. This accounted for *China Youth* and *China Youth Daily*'s respective discussion on the outlook of life in May and July 1980. Society's concern over the discussion was reflected by the 70,000 letters to the editor *China Youth Daily* received within half a year. This was soon acknowledged by the *People's Daily*, which published a commentary titled "Discussion of the Outlook of Life Should be Valued" on July 29. Further on, *Beijing Daily* defended Communism by issuing the commentary "Egoism is Not Human Nature" on January 9, 1981.

As campaigns set out to promote the building of "Socialist spiritual civilization" throughout the nation, the news media added impetus by affirmative propaganda. Starting from the 1980s, propaganda on campaigns to learn from Lei Feng, the prototype of a selfless soldier and victim of the Cultural Revolution, and other nationalistic role models was strengthened. The likes of Lei Feng were promoted in an attempt to reintroduce the virtues of altruism, collectivism, and Communism, which were jeopardized by the money mania and individualism born out of the Reform and Opening Up era. On March 5, 1981, *China Youth Daily* published the editorial "Revisiting Lei Feng," which refuted the arguments that the "Lei Feng spirit" was outdated, too leftist, and contrary to individual values.[15] On the day of its release, the article was immediately reprinted in full by the *Beijing Daily* and excerpted under the title "Yet Greater Necessity for Promoting Lei Feng Spirit in the 80s" in the *People's Daily*.

The number of news stories on exemplary characters and communities during the decade was novel in the history of the People's Republic of China. Model CPC members included PLA hero Zhu Boru, wheelchair intellectual Zhang Haidi, opticist Jiang Zhuying, and microelectronics scientist Luo Jianfu, whereas their collective counterparts included the national women's volleyball team and the voluntary Hua Shan rescue team of 1983.[16] Learning from past experience, news propaganda on these inspiring characters and groups demonstrated considerable improvements:

- Living role models were glorified alongside martyred, sacrificed, or deceased heroes. For example, Zhu Boru and Zhang Haidi were lauded as the "new Lei Fengs of the 1980s."

- Attention was given to both the width and depth of reporting. Long features and creative non-fiction, which were believed to be space-consuming and ineffective, gave way to express news that covered multiple role models. Various forms of news writing were adopted to ensure the prolonged exposure of the same characters. As an example, *Guangming Daily* devoted more than a month to Jiang Zhuying following his immature death starting from October 10, featuring stories and memorial articles about him almost every day. It was these news stories, together with those of the similarly-fated Luo Jianfu, that prompted Hu Qiaomu to write the article "Wishes beyond Lamentation," where he called for concern over the conditions of China's living intellectuals.

- Emphasis was placed on model intellectuals. Not only was the coverage expanded, such propaganda was often placed in the prominent positions of newspapers. Declaring its commitment to let the nation's intellectuals "sit in the front seats of the newspaper," *Guangming Daily* featured as many as 150 exemplary intellectuals between May and December 1982, most of which were allocated space on the front page; in 1983, the total number of such personalities going into the paper increased to 1,381. As a result of media propaganda, an atmosphere of respect for intellectuals was cultivated, injecting motivation for their contributions to the mission of Socialist modernization.

- A commitment to truthful reporting was shown. The truthful face of the role models was kept while publicizing their lives, contributions, and ideologies, and the arbitrary portrayal — or deification — of immaculate, lofty, generous, and altruistic heroes was abandoned. In addition to invoking reverence, the reporting of credible and approachable images was valued.

- Regular columns and programs were created to commend the "sparkles" in the commoners, such as "Deeds of the Ordinary People".

- Critical journalism was developed and achieved in various forms, ranging from express news to letters and phone calls from readers to commentaries by reporters. Many newspapers opted to expose cases of serious ideological or behavioral breaches of society's moral values in such columns as "Moral Court" and "Social Court." Regarding backward phenomena or uncivilized behavior, however, milder approaches were preferred. One common form was the short satirical column that accepted submissions from readers, often illustrated with cartoons. To reinforce the effects of propaganda, some newspapers juxtaposed role models and negative examples.

Awareness of the law

Cultivating law-abiding citizens was one of the goals in building "Socialist spiritual civilization." Media propaganda on the law increased after the Third Plenary Session of the 11th CPC Central Committee, facilitating the communication of legal knowledge and the law-abiding spirit. Legal newspapers were born and thrived, whereas national newspapers, the Central People's Broadcasting Station, and CCTV all developed columns or programs to publicize the law.

The publicity of legal knowledge and legal education were the chief objectives of news propaganda on the law. It was achieved in columns and programs of such names as "Legal Counsel," "Legal Answers," "Legal Garden," and "Legal Talk for Youngsters" by the print and broadcasting media. Moreover, interesting approaches were selected to present ideological knowledge for the sake of popularization. One preferred form was the reporting of typical criminal cases, which was favored for its educational value and readability. Sensational details of crimes were omitted while commentaries were added to provide concrete, impacting lessons for the masses.

The media was charged with a long list of missions in law-related propaganda. These included:

- Publicizing the Party and government's decisions on the development of Socialist democracy and a sound Socialist legal system;
- Issuing major laws adopted by the NPC;
- Exposing and attacking severe criminal offenses and economic crimes;
- Reporting prototypical cases where legal means were used to facilitate economic work;
- Reporting the progress and experience of the popularization of legal knowledge;
- Reporting prototypical cases of law-abiding struggles against crimes; and
- Reporting outstanding judicial workers.

Educational, scientific, and cultural development

The other aspect of the building of "Socialist spiritual civilization," educational, scientific, and cultural development also gained substantial impetus from news propaganda. Brand new special-interest newspapers were set up while discontinued ones resumed publication; by the end of 1988, 14 educational papers, 88 science and technology papers, 36 cultural papers, and 17 sporting papers had been running throughout China. At the same time, news propaganda on educational, scientific, and cultural development was strengthened in general-interest newspapers. The Central People's Broadcasting Station and CCTV, as well as regional television and radio stations, all increased their broadcasting hours of educational (including teaching), science (including hygiene and health), and cultural (including sports and entertainment) shows.

News propaganda on educational, scientific, and cultural development demonstrated the following characteristics:

- Extensive coverage with diverse content. Guiding principles, policies, and decisions over educational, scientific, and cultural development were publicized alongside progress in related reforms, while exemplary pioneers in these fields were glorified. Moreover, popular sporting, art, and cultural events gained increasing coverage in response to the rising craze for sports and culture.

- The promotion of the linkage between educational, scientific, and cultural development and economic and social advancement. Regarding education, places like Shanxi, Shandong, and Hebei were publicized as role models for their rural schools' contributions to local economic development, and connections between institutions of higher learning and society, realized through the integration of teaching, scientific research, and social practice, were promoted. For propaganda on scientific development, the focus fell on how practical science and technology boosted production. Apart from the latest agricultural and industrial technologies and experiences, specific schemes and undertakings such as the Spark Program for disseminating modern technology in rural areas, government funds for aiding the poor with technology, and up-and-coming private technology enterprises all became hot news of the period. In view of the growth of the commodity economy, science and technology newspapers created multitudinous columns for information and communications technology, making technological and market information a leading channel for translating science and technology into productivity. Some science and technology papers even went as far as to organize training classes, taught classes, and specialized schools of new technology. Finally, cultural propaganda was conducted through stories on economic-cum-cultural bodies, as well as the thriving cultures of enterprises, colleges, military camps, communities, and rural villages written from the angle of their benefits to economic and social development.

- The fostering of the cultivation of ideological and moral values through promoting educational, scientific, and cultural development. To counteract the subsidence of ideological and political education as well as political work teams during the Cultural Revolution, renewed efforts on the part of institutions of higher learning were given great publicity. Also promoted were patriotic education, moral education, education on revolutionary traditions, labor education, and legal education in primary and secondary schools. Moreover, news reports of cultural development often departed from an ideological, moral point of view.

- The organization of community activities in support of the development of educational, scientific, and cultural undertakings. Examples included the selection of the National Top Ten Athletes, National Outstanding Class Teachers, and National Outstanding Nurses; sporting events like the National Women's Invitational Football Tournament, Round-the-City Race, and International Youth Invitational Football Tournament; and knowledge contests to boost the reading atmosphere among the masses. There were also all kinds of art and cultural events, such as the CCTV Young Singers Contest, the Chinese Television Flying Apsaras Award, and the Tao Li Cup Chinese dance competition. The influence of the "Love China, Restore Our Great Wall" campaign that called on nationwide donations even extended beyond China. In addition to facilitating educational, scientific, and cultural development, these activities also brought the masses closer to the news industry and increased the reputation of the news units.

The expansion of the watchdog role

Despite the dominance of the propagandist function, the supervisory role of the news media was relatively well-developed during the New Era when compared with prior periods of PRC history. Within the framework of official sanction, the media monitored the work of the Party and the government on behalf of the masses, acting as a bridge between the leadership and the people. Achievements in the supervision by the news media and public opinion were observed in three main aspects:

Improvements in critical journalism

The Cultural Revolution had stirred up tides of "revolutionary great criticism" in the news media following 1957, which obliterated any forms of critical journalism as approved by the *Decision on the Initiation of Criticism and Self-Criticism in Newspapers and Publications* (*Guanyu zai baozhi kanwu shang zhankai piping he ziwo piping de jueding* 關於在報紙刊物上展開批評和自我批評的決

定) at the founding of the People's Republic of China. For this reason, the CPC Central Committee reiterated in its *Decision of the CPC Central Committee on the Current Principles of Propaganda through Newspapers, Publications, and News Broadcasters* (*Zhonggong zhongyang guanyu dangqian baokan xinwen guangbo xuanchuan fangzhen de jueding* 中共中央關於當前報刊新聞廣播宣傳方針的決定) that Party committees at all levels should leverage newspapers and periodicals to provoke criticisms that would be constructive to the work of local governments. Nonetheless, owing to the devastations to social and party traditions during the Cultural Revolution, coupled with the lingering fear and abomination over the "revolutionary great criticism," a lot of obstacles had to be overcome in the reintroduction of critical journalism.

It was with the rebuilding of the economy, the legal system, and "Socialist spiritual civilization" that critical journalism gradually expanded. News reports on the East-West Water Transfer Project and Bohai 2 Disaster in 1980 were prototypical of their kind. It was Xinhua that took the lead in disclosing the postponement of Xiyang County's manpower-and-resource-consuming East-West Water Transfer Project alongside the policy errors committed by the county Party committee's paternalistic outgoing leader on June 14, 1980. This exposure of a once untouchable "exemplary role model" soon released a tide of journalistic criticisms. On the next day, the *People's Daily* published an editorial titled "Never Repeat the Stupidity of East-West Water Transfer," which broke the anti-Dazhai taboo and looked into the common problems faced by agriculture under the shadow of ultra-leftism.[17]

In the same spirit, the *People's Daily* and *Workers' Daily* reported the capsizing of the Bohai No. 2 drillship on July 22, 1980. The *Workers' Daily* went a step further by issuing a separate investigative article titled "What the Bohai No. 2 Drillship Sinking Disaster Revealed" on the same day, debunking the Marine Petroleum Exploration Bureau of the Ministry of Petroleum's attempt to cover up its mistaken, rule-breaking leadership that had led to the fatal accident on November 25, 1979. This was followed by an eight-month investigation by several news units in the capital, which ended in the full exposure of the details of the accident and the flaws of the Ministry of Petroleum. On August 25, 1980, Xinhua reported the State Council's verdict over the disaster. The host of letters to the editor praising the uncommon practices of the dismissal of the minister, penalization of the deputy-minister, and open evaluation by the State Council attested to the public's enthusiasm for the final ruling.

The coverage of the East-West Water Transfer Project and Bohai 2 Disaster exemplified three aspects of breakthroughs in critical journalism: The first breakthrough was the unprecedented approval of the disclosure of major accidents, including those caused by negligence and policy errors. The State Council stated in its resolution to the Bohai 2 Disaster, "All major accidents must be reported truthfully in time, without any concealment or distortion." This led to truthful and immediate media coverage of major accidents thereafter, including the 1987 Daxing'anling wildfire, the 1988 Shanghai hepatitis A epidemic, and various transportation accidents. The second breakthrough was the open criticism of the flaws of the previously deified, inviolable role models. The third was the gradual disintegration of the taboo of criticism against senior Party cadres. The October after the Bohai 2 Disaster, the *People's Daily*, *China Youth Daily*, and Central People's Broadcasting Station reported and commented on the Central Commission for Discipline Inspection's issuing of criticism against Minister of Commerce Wang Lei's underpayment at a restaurant. In addition to enhancing the reform and development of the economic and legal systems, the groundbreaking reporting of the two incidents also had the effect of increasing the reputation of the Party and the news media, which in turn motivated journalists to make constructive criticisms.

The extension of the scope of supervision by the news media and public opinion
Following the Third Plenary Session of the 11th CPC Central Committee, the scope of supervision gradually stretched to the political, economic, and cultural aspects of life. The targets of supervision ranged from Party and state organs to various sectors of society, while in terms of content, policy resolutions, the government's work, the law, and social moral standards all came under scrutiny.

Regarding the monitoring of policy resolutions, the news media looked into the feasibility of reform policies and circulated opinions given by various sectors of society. A remarkable example was the publication of practical opinions from NPC and CPPCC (Chinese People's Political Consultative Conference) delegates during the two meetings since the 1980s. Generally speaking, policies that gained wide media attention included major reforms (such as the price reform, economic reform, and labor reform) and construction projects (such as South-North Water Transfer and Yangtze Three Gorges).

Media supervision of the government's work concerned problems in actual policy implementation, aiming at ensuring that approved policies were properly carried out by cadres at all levels of government. As for law-related supervision, an important role of the news media was to involve the public in the process of legislation through information provision, such as by the detailed news coverage of the NPC's discussions during the legislation of the *Enterprise Bankruptcy Law* (*Qiye pochan fa* 企業破產法) in 2006. Moreover, to raise public awareness of the law, compliance to the law on the part of state organs and cadres at all levels, especially of the leadership, was frequently commended, while infringements of the law were reprimanded. Substantial attention was given to cases of corruption, which undesirably grew and spread with the advancement of Reform and Opening Up.

Finally, the supervision of society's moral standards went hand in hand with propaganda on the building of "Socialist spiritual civilization," resulting in educational criticisms against behavior that fell short of the expected moral standards, for example, the maltreatment of senior citizens, women, and children.

The enhancement of the media's bridging role, both between the masses and the government and among the masses

A product of the Third Plenary Session of the 11th CPC Central Committee other than the economic reform was the steady reform of the political system. The 13th CPC Central Committee in 1987 yielded the slogan "From the masses, to the masses," the pledge to increase the openness and transparency of the leadership, and the acknowledgement of public discussion of important issues. These denoted the respect and further guarantee of the public's right to know, to speak, and to supervise. The spectrum of news reporting benefited from the leadership's gradually increasing openness. News stories on political and Party affairs like the NPC, CPPCC, and CPC Central Committee meetings became more detailed, concrete, and comprehensive. Eventually, the meetings, group discussions, and press conferences of these high-level state bodies began to enter public knowledge through live television and radio broadcasts. A supportive gesture from the government was the establishment of a news spokesperson system in the State Council and many government departments, which enabled state organs to inform the public of important policies and news as well as to answer questions of public concern through the media.

The news media reflected the quests of the public in two main aspects: first, by immersing among the masses, so as to gain real understanding into people's lives and speak for the people; and second, by publishing letters and articles written by the commoners that made commendations, criticisms, suggestions, complaints, and charges. While letters and articles from readers were often published in excerpts, it was common practice for organizations to forward them to relevant government leaders or departments in full. The *People's Daily*, *Workers' Daily*, and *Nanfang Daily* ran the best "Letters to the Editor," which had by then become a familiar section to the general newspaper readership. Alongside the efforts of the print media, television and radio stations were enthusiastic in developing programs like *Readers' Mailbox* (*Tingzhong xinxiang* 聽眾信箱) and *The Screen and the Audience* (*Pingmu yu guanzhong* 屏幕與觀眾).

From such experience during the New Era, we can derive the following principles for the implementation of media and public opinion supervision in China: First, journalists must stand by the interests of both the Party and the people. Media and public opinion supervision must be understood as supervision on the part of the people instead of the isolated efforts of individual journalists or news units, and it should not go as far as to embrace such freedom of the press as advocated by the bourgeois liberals. Second was the importance of investigation in order to ensure the truthfulness of the news reports. This refers not only to the truthful and accurate representation of single incidents, but also truthfulness in terms of the overall picture, the quintessence of the question involved, and the developmental trends. Third, the media should leverage the motivating power of the news, selecting resolvable issues of popular interest in order to optimize the effects of public opinion supervision. Fourth, the support of the CPC and the government was key to the effectiveness of public opinion supervision. Fifth, media and public opinion supervision must be contained within the boundaries of the constitution and the law; organizations and journalists must be subject to the supervision of the Party and the people.

As seen, there was considerable progress in the development of media and public opinion supervision a decade into the New Era. However, it should always be remembered that the period only marked a beginning. More experience had yet to be accumulated for this watchdog role to be taken to the nect level.

World news and news reporting for international audiences

The opening up of China signified the increase of interactions between the nation and the outside world in all aspects. This meant a pressing need on the part of China to understand the drastically-changing international landscape. Nations and regions around the globe, in response, were as eager to find out about the latest scene of the reforming party-state. Against this backdrop, the reporting of world news in China and the release of domestic news to international audiences bloomed with never-before-seen momentum, adding to the prosperity of journalism during the New Era.

World news

The popularity of world news among China's news audiences was evident.

According to a sampling survey conducted by the Beijing Journalism Studies Society in 1982, world news topped the list of readers' favorite topics.[18] In 1986, the *People's Daily*'s readers' survey showed that world news ranked third in terms of popularly, preceded only by political and legal news.[19] The circulation of *Reference News* (*Cankao xiaoxi* 參考消息), a daily published by Xinhua which focused on world news, went up to seven million in 1981, and in 1989, in spite of the improvement and expansion of the world news section of all sorts of news media, the paper still sold at a rate of five million copies per day, surpassing the circulation of all dailies. Looking at the corresponding figures of radio broadcasting, the Central People's Broadcasting Station's *World News and Current Affairs* (*Guoji xinwen yu shishi* 國際新聞與時事) recorded a rating of 83.29%; 79.94% of the station's audience expressed that they liked the program, making it the listeners' third favorite program.[20]

Improvements and reinforcement in the reporting of world news during the New Era were materialized in the two main aspects:

First, the substantial increase in the amount of world news, and the improvement in the timeliness of reporting. During the Cultural Revolution, when news publications and programs were manipulated for power usurpation, world news was next to non-existent. The situation was rectified with the introduction of the Reform and Opening Up policy. Subsequently, two out of eight pages of the *People's Daily* were set apart for world news, which also supplied readers with fundamental knowledge of the outside world. Xinhua started reforming its world news reporting section in 1980, which resulted in 49,436 English releases of world news in 1989, or 135.4 per day on average.[21]

CCTV started broadcasting world news from Visnews and UPITN (United Press International Television News) received through communications satellites in April 1980, enabling the Chinese to keep pace with the world with only a day's time lag. Another move of CCTV was the incorporation of *World News* (*Guoji xinwen* 國際新聞) into *Xinwen Lianbo* 新聞聯播 (literally "news simulcast"), turning the latter into a program that offered comprehensive coverage of domestic and external affairs. Moreover, the broadcaster increased the portion of news on Taiwan, Hong Kong, Macau, and certain countries or regions that had members in the Asia-Pacific Broadcasting Union. At the time of the writing of this book, it is able to receive world news and major international events by communications satellites and provide live broadcasts when necessary.

The Central People's Broadcasting Station and China Radio International (CRI) proved especially timely in the reporting of sudden international events. Their excellence was also reflected in the number of world news pieces reported. To take

China Radio International as an example, it broadcast as many as 12,801 world news items in 1988, meaning 35 every day, among which 5,040 were sourced from the station's own foreign correspondents.

Second, the upholding of the principles of objectivity, fairness, truthfulness, and comprehensiveness. As early as May 28, 1956, Liu Shaoqi expressed in a discussion about Xinhua: "The Xinhua News Agency has to be a world news agency. News releases from the Xinhua News Agency must be objective, truthful, fair, and comprehensive, yet at the same time come with a stance."[22] These principles were brought down to the New Era. Examples of "truth-reflecting news reporting with a clear point of view" included stories on U.S. arms sales to Taiwan, and the Japanese Ministry of Education, Science and Culture's approval of textbooks that distorted the history of Japan's militarist invasion. Likewise, regarding the eight-year Iran-Iraq War in the 1980s, the Chinese news media always put forward the government's stance of wanting a ceasefire and peace talks alongside objective reports. Concurrently, denunciation was made against such hegemonism, colonialism, and racism as was revealed in the U.S. bombing of Libya, the dispatch of the British Task Force to the Falklands, the Soviet military attack of Afghanistan, and the South African apartheid policies.

The principle of comprehensiveness was realized in the regional distribution of nations or regions covered, and the content of news stories. News on third world countries and capitalist nations paralleled, stretching beyond political and foreign affairs to cover economic, cultural, and social issues. In fact, the simultaneous reporting of both the bright and dark sides of developed countries — from economic and technological advancement to economic recession and social problems, such as criminal offenses, drug abuse, and the spread of AIDS — manifested how comprehensive reporting tied in with the spirit of objectivity, fairness, and truthfulness. Moreover, the Chinese news media showed great enthusiasm in reporting major sports, art, and cultural events around the globe, including the Olympics, the FIFA World Cup, and many renowned film festivals on the one hand, while increasing their coverage of catastrophes outside China. News of the American Space Shuttle Challenger Disaster, the Russian Chernobyl Disaster, major transportation accidents, natural disasters, and large-scale environmental pollution reached the Chinese audience soon after their occurrence.

Limitations in China's world news reporting, nonetheless, should not be camouflaged by the noted achievements. For instance, in addition to reporting the progress in East-West Détente, more attention should have been given to the rising tension between the North and the South (i.e., between capitalist and developing countries). News reports on the developed capitalist nations should have been accompanied by more comprehensive and in-depth investigations. Last but not least was the delayed development of world news commentaries, which appeared particularly scanty and substandard given the plenitude of corresponding news stories.

News reporting for international audiences

News reporting for international audiences, or *duiwai baodao* 對外報導 (literally external reporting), was held as a display window into China's progress in Socialist modernization to the outside world. Achievements in news reporting for international audiences can be summarized in four aspects:

The first was the development of specific media channels serving international audiences. Media corporations charged with the mission of reporting for international audiences included the Xinhua News Agency, China News Service, China Radio International, CCTV, the Central People's Broadcasting Station (Taiwan Service), the *People's Daily (Overseas Edition)*, and *China Daily* (*Zhongguo ribao* 中國日報). The establishment of the last two was particularly central to the overall enhancement of news reporting to the outside world. The role of Xinhua, risen to a seat among the world's top six news agencies, was evident. It offered news dispatches in five languages other than Chinese (English, French, Spanish, Arabic, and Russian) every day. The other news agency in the list, China News Service, targeted overseas Chinese, ethnic Chinese with foreign nationalities, as well as Chinese in Hong Kong, Macau, and Taiwan. Its expansion was acknowledged by UNESCO's awarding of the B grade in 1982. China Radio International broadcast in 43 languages for a total of 140 hours every day, ranking third among the world's external broadcasting services both in the number of languages and total broadcasting hours. CCTV kept pace with the times by introducing English programs, releasing dispatches to the Asia-Pacific Broadcasting Union, offering television programs to foreign and overseas Chinese-language television stations, and developing new channels for supplying satellite news to One World Channel in Western Europe and programs to CNN. The Central People's Broadcasting Station increased the number of programs tailored for Taiwan to two per day. The prosperity of such media channels witnessed the modernization of the means of news reporting, expanding the size of international audiences of China news.

The second aspect was the increase in overall competitiveness. To begin with, the Reform and Opening Up policy gave rise to a surge in the amount of news reporting for international audiences. Taking Xinhua's English releases for instance, the average daily number grew from 17 in 1982 to 24.7 in 1983, 35 in 1986, and then 41.5 in 1989. China News Service also distributed as many as around 30 press releases per day and 300 features, dispatches, column articles, and supplement articles per month to the international media. Regarding the press, the *People's Daily (Overseas Edition)* maintained an average of 15 stories on each page of its news section since it was established in 1985. Another factor that motivated improvements was the increasing awareness of competition, and the gradual modernization of news competition, which led to more timely news releases. Lastly, competitiveness increased with the expansion of the scope of reporting. An aspect of this was the balanced reporting of both positive and negative news in order to provide an overall picture that reflected China's achievements and problems amid its Reform and Opening Up. The overall scope of news reporting was also stretched to the major fields of politics, economics, culture, and society. Economic news, for example, then included finance, energy, transportation, and foreign trade. More efforts were made to introduce China's history, famous personalities, culture and art, scenic spots and attractions, as well as local customs to the outside world.

The third achievement had to do with the customized and diverse styles of reporting. Because of the diversity of target audiences, the news media adopted varying approaches that catered to the needs and concerns of specific countries and regions. Customized reporting was carried out in two respects: first, reporting China news according to the characteristics and needs of target countries and regions; second, helping people outside China gain a comprehensive understanding of the nation in times of major national conferences, major policy enactment, and important events according to their concerns. To make it plain, a large part of the second aspect was to communicate China's position over sensitive issues to the outside world. The Chinese media's reaction after the Tiananmen Square protests of 1989 was a good example: in defense of their country's image, news units consistently portrayed the incident as a riot stirred up by the minority against a legal Chinese government. Afterwards, positive news reports on the recovery of social order, steady economic development, and the coherence of the Chinese nationals under the helm of Jiang Zemin were put forward as remedies of the nation's impaired reputation.

Regarding the diversity of styles in news reporting for international audiences, the reading, listening, and television habits of audiences outside China were taken into account in the design of columns and programs. Each news unit demonstrated unique strengths and creativity. Xinhua's strength was the diversity in the forms of reporting, which included commentaries, profiles, serial stories, regional stories, travel notes, and opinion polls. China News Service was characterized by its influential political and economic commentaries. Broadcasting in numerous languages, China Radio International increased its proportion of participatory programs, audio news, audio interviews, and current affairs programs. The Central People's Broadcasting Station (Taiwan Service) started adopting the radio-host style in the program *Friend in the Air* (*Kongzhong zhi you* 空中之友), which conferred to its host Xu Man's fame as the most popular "Air Hostess" from the Mainland in Taiwan. The *People's Daily (Overseas Edition)* had the most special issues and columns among China's major newspapers. Its succinct and vivid headlines, combined with refreshing layout of news photographs and graphs, won the hearts of the overseas readers. Lastly, *China Daily* was directly written in English, characterized by the use of large pictures, and arranged according to the tastes of overseas readers.

The last characteristic was the focus on the questions of Taiwan, Hong Kong, and Macau. The Chinese news media always promoted patriotism in reporting for international audiences, advocating One Country, Two Systems as a formula for unification. Regarding Taiwan, the CPC's principles and policies were presented in commentaries and news summaries, while the development of cross-Strait relations, and opinions from the island and overseas were reflected in news stories. Taiwanese initiatives to improve cross-Strait relations, for example, the policies that allowed Taiwan residents to visit their family on the Mainland in 1987, permitted Mainland citizens to visit sick relatives and attend funerals in Taiwan in 1988, and relaxed restrictions on imports from the Mainland in the same year, were given substantial coverage. On the other hand, pro-independence gestures, including the advocacy of the Three-Noes policy, the "friend-enemy distinction," the Two Chinas or One China, One Taiwan resolution, the double recognition of China and Taiwan, and "flexible diplomacy" were criticized. In any case, the stance of the Party prevailed: zero foreign intervention, and the preference for peaceful unification without abandoning the right to use military force.

News coverage on Hong Kong and Macau revolved around the principles of One Country, Two Systems and peaceful unification, as well as the progress of negotiations with the United Kingdom and Portugal. As the drafting of the Basic Law kicked off in Hong Kong and Macau, the media's lens closely followed. The *People's Daily (Overseas Edition)* set up a special column called "HKSAR Basic Law (Draft) Discussion," which published dozens of articles in total.

Also coming under the limelight was the economic aspect of the Hong Kong,

Macau, and Taiwan question. Added attention was given to Taiwan's investments in Mainland China, and the mushrooming indirect business dealings between the two sides of the Strait. The *People's Daily (Overseas Edition)* published 20 articles under the specially created column "Pen Talks on Strengthening Mainland-Hong Kong-Macau Economic Relations." Moreover, cross-Strait interactions of all kinds, from the Three Links of direct postal, transportation, and trade to such activities as relatives visiting, tourism, and art, cultural, sporting, and academic events, were frequently reported to foster the Mainland-Taiwan tie. Hence, the reporting of Taiwan, Hong Kong, and Macau news for international audiences was essentially externally-oriented news propaganda on peaceful unification.

News propaganda on China's economic opening

The Third Plenary Session of the 11th CPC Central Committee was an economic watershed for China. As far as news propaganda was concerned, the pivotal economic opening policy was a key component.

To provide a quick overview of Deng's economic opening of China, the policy advanced in two main phases, based on the rationale that the initially developed regions would eventually drive the development of their late-starting counterparts. The first step was completed between 1979 and 1988, which materialized in the establishment of five Special Economic Zones, namely, Shenzhen, Zhuhai, Shantou, Xiamen, and Hainan, which were relatively backward areas neighboring Hong Kong, Macau, and Taiwan. Success was slowly pieced together over a decade, as the foreign-invested "processing and assembly factory business" (or *san lai yi bu* 三來 一補, short for processing with supplied materials, processing according to supplied designs, assembling with supplied parts, and compensation trade) gradually developed into foreign direct investment and the introduction of advanced technology and management.

Then came the second step in 1990, touched off by the development of the Shanghai Pudong New Area. With a focus in tertiary industries (mainly business, commerce, finance, information, and technology), the establishment of Pudong also denoted the commencement of industry development.

Returning to news propaganda on the economic opening of China, five characteristics could be observed:

First, different, yet related focuses for internal and external propaganda. Internal propaganda aimed at publicizing the strategic significance of the country's opening up to Socialist modernization, getting across the principles, policies, laws, and regulations of the opening up policy, reporting the progress and achievements of opening up, and promoting corresponding exemplary experiences. Confusion brought by the Cultural Revolution, which left behind queries as to whether the act of opening up would turn China into a capitalist state, made ideological clarification among the cadres and masses all the more important. Substantially speaking, the news media propagated Deng's theory of Socialism with Chinese characteristics, including the differentiation between Socialism and capitalism, and the relationship between opening up and self-reliance, while at the same time closely following the development of the Special Economic Zones.

External propaganda targeted not only overseas countries, but also Hong Kong, Macau, and Taiwan, as these places had shown particular concern over the permanency of the opening up policy and whether foreign enterprises in China would be nationalized. The purpose of propaganda, naturally, was to boost external confidence in the long-term stability of the new policy.

Second, the use of policy propaganda. Besides promoting the overall principles of the opening up policy, the news media also kept the public updated on progressively released policies and laws and regulations, often proclaimed and explicated through speeches of government leaders. Facing the outside world, it played an important role in wielding public opinion against Western suspicions that China was to abandon Reform and Opening Up in critical times, such as during the Anti-Spiritual Pollution Campaign of 1983, the Anti-Bourgeois Liberalism Campaign in 1986, and the suppression of the 1989 protests.

Third, the strengthened coverage of reform prototypes. The media's focus fell on such Special Economic Zones as Shenzhen, an archetype of the economic reform. After the establishment of the Shenzhen Special Economic Zone in 1979, abundant news stories were presented to relate the progress of the city's developments. Publicity was given to the city's implementation of the special economic policy; the evolution of its diverse economic structure, where economic development leveraged mainly on foreign capital yet ownership remained public; the dynamics of its economic activities, which were simultaneously regulated by the state's macroeconomic policy and adjusted by the market; the details of its preferential policies for foreign investors; and its expanded power in economic management. Before 1985, the building of a favorable investment environment for infrastructural construction was put in the spotlight, whereas after 1986, media coverage was stretched to the full-fledged development of the external-oriented economy with industry at the center, surrounded by commerce, agriculture, and tourism. Apart from taking a macro approach to the development of the Special Economic Zones, the news media also zoomed in on the three types of foreign-invested enterprises (enterprises based on foreign investment, Chinese-foreign joint-ventures, and Chinese-foreign joint management ventures), which concerned people outside China most.

Fourth, the reporting of problems in the implementation of the opening up policy. As far as the disclosure of problems was concerned, the following principles were observed:

- In the reporting of general problems related to economic opening up, a cautious approach was taken with neither concealment nor exaggeration.
- Problems caused by the lack of experience or inherited from the old economic system were restrainedly reported with carefully chosen perspectives, timing, and forms. In order not to cause panic, they were portrayed as problems in the course of development that could be resolved through practical experience and further reforms.
- In the face of conflicts caused by the responsibility of one party, analyses were made on the basis of equality and mutual benefit.

That said, it was propaganda that dominated news coverage of China's economic opening up. Achievements in the refinement of the legal system, the improvement of the investment environment, the development of foreign-invested enterprises, and the proclamation of new measures were vehemently publicized to demonstrate China's determination and capacity in opening up to the outside world.

Fifth, the publicity of the opening up of the inland and bordering areas. The windows and samples of China's opening up to the outside world, the coastal Special Economic Zones had been the center stage of news propaganda from the beginning. However, they were more starting points than destinations of the country's economic reform. Soon, the news media took on the new mission of publicizing the impact of economic opening up on the inland and bordering areas. In this, particularity was the catchword. Instead of unleashing news reports on all places in a flood, the media put out propaganda articles, always tailored to local situations, in the order of the opening up of these areas. Experiences of the first developed areas were publicized as lessons for references rather than rules, while localized focuses and approaches of opening up were highlighted.

As many places in the inland and along the border were rather unknown to the outside world, an important goal of such news propaganda was to increase their international exposure. To invoke a sense of locality, the geography, transportation, raw materials, agricultural and industrial products, economic distinctiveness, tourist attractions and historical relics, as well as culture and customs of various places were publicized around the nexus of external economic relations. Very often, this was achieved by reporting events and activities that integrated economic interactions with art, culture, sports, or tourism, such as the Weifang International Kite Festival in Shandong, Zigong International Dinosaur Lantern Festival in Sichuan, and China Wuqiao International Circus Festival in Hebei.

In order to draw in foreign capital for the opening up of inland and bordering areas, the news media highlighted improvements in the investment environment of these places, especially features of the soft environment, such as simplified work procedures, high work efficiency, a sound economic system, superior public services, and a good social order.

Struggles against bourgeois liberalism

The period between the spring and summer of 1989 was a tumultuous time for the CPC. To the single-party state, the political turmoil leading up to the protests at the start of the summer amounted to a counterrevolutionary revolt against the Communist leadership and the Socialist system. In retrospect, the dissenting opinions stemmed from the intricate social and historical backgrounds following the Second World War.

In view of the international environment, the scientific and technological revolution brought by the world war had significantly strengthened the economies of the capitalist world. Coincidentally, due to policy flaws, many Socialist states were wading through a socioeconomic trough. Socialism thus was caught between these starkly contrasting two sides of the modern world. As the capitalist powers heightened their strength in driving the strategy of "peaceful evolution," beliefs about the inferiority of Socialism began to spread among the intellectuals, students, and even party members of Socialist countries. China was far from immune to these international currents.

Domestically speaking, a yearning for such liberalism and democracy as were advocated by the capitalist states began to surface after the smashing of the Gang of Four. Alarmed by such signs of bourgeois liberalism, Deng Xiaoping professed the Party's position through his newly-crafted Four Cardinal Principles, put forth in the Forum on the Principles for Theoretical Work in March 1979: the upholding of the Socialist path, the people's democratic dictatorship, the leadership of the CPC, as well as Marxism-Leninism and Mao Zedong Thought. However, efforts like the Anti-Spiritual Pollution Campaign and Anti-Bourgeois Liberalism

Campaign failed to contain the proliferation of contrary sentiments. Widespread political turmoil finally broke out.

The devastations of the rise of bourgeois liberalism to the CPC were reflected in the deviation of some news media from the Party line. This was deemed a severe wrongdoing committed by the news media, which gave the media the most important lesson since the implementation of the Reform and Opening Up policy.

The emergence and development of bourgeois liberalism in the journalism sector

As mentioned, the Third Plenary Session of the 11th CPC Central Committee created polarized responses in addition to the mainstream ideology that concentrated on the eradication of personality cults and dogmatism. The opposite extreme of the continuous adherence to leftism was the negation of Communist leadership and Socialism, what had come to be regarded as bourgeois liberalism. Under the banners of social reforms and the emancipation of the mind, followers of this school of thought instigated protests using such slogans as "down with hunger" and "up with human rights, democracy, and liberalism." Certain members of the CPC went along with this wave of thought, showing direct or indirect support for the bourgeois liberals.

It was in the same meeting where the Four Cardinal Principles were announced that dissenting bourgeois liberal opinions rose to the fore. These opinions can be summarized in three points:

- The righting of ultra-leftism together with the righting of Socialism; the belief that Socialism should not be practiced too soon, and lessons should be borrowed from capitalism.
- The righting of Mao's wrongs in his old age and the negation of Mao Zedong Thought.
- The advocacy of democracy, liberalism, and human rights above the Communist notion of people's democratic dictatorship.

Such thoughts were echoed by some in the journalism field. In the 1979 National Journalism Seminar, some sought to differentiate between the "Party spirit" (*dang xing* 黨性) and the "people spirit" (*renmin xing* 人民性) through debates on the nature of Party newspapers. There were calls for absolute freedom of the press, to be realized through a diverse structure that tolerated private newspapers, as opposed to the monopoly of Party newspapers. Journalists were to be "conscious subjects" awakening to individual emancipation. Journalism theories from the West were cited to advance the diversification of the news media away from its primary role as the mouthpiece of the Party and the government, i.e., a tool for publicizing government principles and policies. A representative example of media advocacy of bourgeois liberalism was CCTV's repeated broadcasting of the documentary series *River Elegy* (*He shang* 河殤) in 1988, which portrayed the inferiority of traditional Chinese culture when compared with Western ideas. Essentially, all these were attempts to establish journalism as an independent force apart from the authority of Party leadership after the fashion of Western capitalist states.

Media perpetuation of pro-bourgeois liberal opinions

While the majority of news units adhered to the Party spirit during the 1989 protests, some went the other way, publicizing public opinion that was unfavorable to the Party.

The protests were triggered by the death of former General Secretary Hu Yaobang on April 15, 1989, after which the mourning activities quickly turned into a student movement. Posters and slogans attacking the high officials, the leadership of the CPC, and the Socialist system pervaded university campuses. Political demands with a long-term agenda, the most important being the reversion of anti-bourgeois liberalism and the rehabilitation of those criticized or penalized for their liberalistic cause, were put forward. In the first 10 days following the death of Hu, some news media encouraged bourgeois liberal quests by taking an objective approach to reporting rather than standing by the Party line.

The *People's Daily* tried to hold back the commotion by writing back in the statement-making editorial "Strong Hold Against Riots a Must" on April 26: "This is a planned conspiracy, a riot that seeks to negate the leadership of the Communist Party of China from the quintessence, and to negate the Socialist system." After May 4, 80% of the students on strike returned to school; however, when the then General Secretary Zhao Ziyang delivered a speech that contradicted the stance of the CPC Central Committee at a meeting with international delegates who came for a board of directors' meeting of the Asian Development Bank, newspapers sympathetic to the students brought the speech to the forefront of coverage with unusual enthusiasm.

The sympathetic media paid no more heed to the Party's instruction to stand firm against the protesters after the outbreak of the hunger strike in Tiananmen Square on May 13. On the contrary, much of the news media placed the strike in the center of their lens, fueling anti-government feelings through extensive coverage and sentimental language. Some continued to speak for the opponents even after martial law was declared on May 20, and past the ultimate military suppression on June 4.

Lessons for Socialist journalism

In the context of Socialist journalism, the news media that sided with the protesters during the 1989 political turmoil fell totally short of their expected role in keeping public opinion close to the Party line. Lessons from the political disaster included:

- Keeping the leadership of Socialist journalism in the firm grip of unswerving Marxists. The relaxation by such leaders as Zhao Ziyang was believed to be the major cause that provided room for deviations. The "leadership of Socialist journalism" referred not only to the Party Central Committee's command of news reporting and public opinion, but also its headship over each news unit.
- Reinstating the media's role as the mouthpiece of the Party, the government, and the people, and their primary missions of publicizing the Party's principles and policies.
- Maintaining the proletarian Party spirit, i.e., the belief of the oneness of the "Party spirit" and the "people spirit," in journalism.
- Strictly abiding by the political direction of Socialism in any reform of journalism.
- Strengthening the political, ideological, practical, and organizational foundations of journalists through the extensive education of the fundamental Marxist theory and Marxist journalism theory, the national situation, the law, discipline, and professional ethics.

The restoration of positive propaganda

Positive propaganda returned to dominance again after the suppression of the 1989 protests.

On June 9, Deng Xiaoping expressed in an address to officials at or above the rank of general in command of the troops enforcing martial law in Beijing: "The outbreak of this incident has given us much food for thought, impelling us to reflect soberly on the past and the future. Perhaps this bad thing will enable us … to correct our errors more quickly and give better play to our advantages."[23] The Fourth Plenary Session of the 13th CPC Central Committee arrived at a conclusion about the Party's future principles and missions following the restoration of order. The guideline of "one central task and two basic points" was to be the backbone of

China's development strategy: the nation should advance economic development on the basis of further economic reforms together with the Four Cardinal Principles.

In November 1989, Jiang Zemin and Li Ruihuan spoke on behalf of the CPC Central Committee in a seminar on journalism organized by the Propaganda Department. With the topics "Several Issues Concerning the Party's Journalism Work" and "Persist with the Principle of Positive Propaganda," respectively, they explicated the Party's view on journalism in numerous aspects, including:

- The role and functions of journalism;
- The basic principles of journalism;
- The Party spirit in journalism;
- The freedom of the press;
- The matter of truthfulness in news reporting;
- The Party's leadership over journalism;
- The significance of guiding public opinion;
- The value and improvement of critical reporting;
- Appropriate supervision by public opinion;
- The improvement of the quality of the journalists; and
- Strict discipline on news propaganda.

The speeches were given to provide an antidote against the infiltration of bourgeois liberal ideologies.

In the days that followed, the news media that had defected to bourgeois liberalism was recovered, and propagandist journalism was reinstated. The suppression of counterrevolutionary protests, struggle against bourgeois liberalism, deepening of economic reform, strengthening of ideopolitical work, establishment of Socialist democracy and law, and penalization of corruption became hot themes of news propaganda. Details of such initiatives are listed below:

- The denunciation of the 1989 protests as a "counterrevolutionary riot." The *People's Liberation Army Daily*, following the decision of the Central Committee and Central Military Commission, started filling their pages with editorials, commentaries, news stories, and photographs that portrayed the protests as a "counterrevolutionary riot" as soon as midnight of June 4. Starting from June 7, the paper glorified the likes of Cui Guozheng, Liu Guogeng, and Li Quorui as "Guardians of the Republic," role models in the People's Liberation Army who sacrificed their lives for the interests of the nation and the people. During and after the suppression of the protests, when the delivery of newspapers was disrupted in Beijing, the Central People's Broadcasting Station, CCTV, and the Beijing People's Broadcasting Station all increased the broadcasting hours of their newscasts. For CCTV, its *Xinwen Lianbo* was extended from 30 minutes to over an hour, and its news reports were repeated over 10 times per day. It also presented a program created by the headquarters of the troops enforcing martial law, namely, *The Truth of the Riot* (*Baoluan zhenxiang* 暴亂真相). Likewise, the Beijing People's Broadcasting Station looped news, commentaries, and bulletins about the suppression of counterrevolutionary protests round the clock. The *People's Daily* talked back against media outside China in articles like "The Truth of the Outbreak of a Counterrevolutionary Riot in Beijing" and "Peaceful Withdrawal, Zero Death: Interviews with Those Who Cleared Tiananmen Square on June 4."

- The emphatic publicity of the Four Cardinal Principles. In July 1989, the CPC Central Committee issued the *Notice on the Strengthening of Propaganda and Ideopolitical Work* (*Guanyu jiaqiang xuanchuan, sixiang gongzuo de tongzhi* 關於加強宣傳、思想工作的通知). Accordingly, educating the masses, especially the youth, about the Four Cardinal Principles became a central component of news propaganda. Apart from providing theoretical justification for the upholding of the Four Cardinal Principles in China, the media also rebutted attacks against these principles as well as bourgeois liberal quests for democracy, liberation, and human rights. The television series *River Elegy* was fiercely criticized for its appeal to idealism and national nihilism as well as use of dubious historical sources.

- The dynamic publicity of the achievements of the People's Republic of China in its 40-year history. On October 1, 1989, the 40th anniversary of the founding of the PRC (or the first one after the 1989 protests), national and regional news organizations took the opportunity to conduct positive propaganda about the party-state's achievements since its establishment, especially after Reform and Opening Up. CCTV took the lead by creating a news program called *In a Fingersnap* (*Tanzhi yihui jian* 彈指一揮間) during the celebration of the anniversary, which manifested the nation's achievements in various fields of work and in different physical regions. Another example was demonstrated by the *People's Daily*, which set apart an entire page for an anniversary feature titled "Social Undertakings are Advancing" during the period, introducing changes in China's provinces, municipalities, and autonomous regions over the years. Xinhua devoted all its international dispatches to anniversary features, and compiled numerous sets of exhibition photographs, including those grouped under the album *40 Years of the Republic* (*Gongheguo 40 nian* 共和國 40 年), for domestic exhibition and display in overseas embassies. As for radio stations, the Central People's Broadcasting Station and China Radio International, respectively, developed the programs *Sing the Song of Entrepreneurship Again* (*Chongchang chuangye ge* 重唱創業歌) and *40 Years of New China* (*Xin zhongguo 40 nian* 新中國 40 年). China Radio International also hosted a large-scale knowledge contest to arouse people's interest in the PRC's 40 years of history.

- The promotion of economic development as the central task of development. Obstacles that sprang up in the initial stage of the economic reform, such as the troubles of a sluggish market and chain debts, had led to uncertainties about the future of the Reform and Opening Up policy. To quench worries about an undesirable turnaround, economic news stressed the principles of "consistent rectification" and "deepening reform." The *People's Daily* started the new column "Pen Talks on Learning from the Fifth Plenary Session of 13th CPC Central Committee" for the reprinting of officials' and economists' reflections on the *Decision on the Further Rectification and Deepening of Reform* (*Guanyu jinyibu zhili zhengdun he shenhua gaige de jueding* 關於進一步治理整頓和深化改革的決定) adopted in the conference, in addition to publishing editorials and commentaries.

- The rebuilding of the image of the CPC. This was done by publicizing the CPC Central Committee's determination in improving the Party's ethics and probity as well as going out to the masses.

- The publicity of the strengthening of ideopolitical work. The weakening of ideological and political education was regarded as a major cause of the degeneration of morals, as reflected in the spreading of bourgeois ills likes short-term materialism and the blind worship of foreign ideas. Targeting the youth, articles such as *China Youth Daily*'s "China is Poor but Weighty: Interview with Former UN Deputy Secretary-General Comrade Tang Mingzhao," *Beijing Youth Daily* (*Beijing qingnian bao* 北京青年報)'s "Perceiving Student Movements from the Characteristics of University Students," and the *People's Daily*'s "How Well-Intended Patriotic Wishes Went to the Negative Extreme" were published to reinforce ideopolitical education. In addition, the merits of ideological role models were publicized by all channels. The National Conference of Model Workers and Advanced Workers became the subject of the specially-developed "Records of Heroes" section of the Central People's Broadcasting Station's *News and Newspaper Digest* (*Xinwen bao zhai* 新聞

報摘). CCTV showed seven episodes of *For Love of the Republic* (*Gongheguo zhi lian* 共和國之戀) on the eve of the PRC's 40th anniversary, in glorification of the selfless technocrats who had contributed to the modernization of the nation. The initiative of *Sichuan Youth* (*Sichuan qingnian bao* 四川青年報) to publish a long piece of creative non-fiction on a young hero named Lai Ning, followed by its reporting of youth campaigns to learn from him, boosted similar campaigns all over the country. Lastly, the media was as persistent in propagating struggles against the "six evils" of prostitution, pornography, the kidnapping of women and children, drug addiction, gambling, and superstition.

Progress in the Development of Journalism Industries after the Third Plenary Session of the 11th CPC Central Committee

Ideological struggles aside, China's journalism industries experienced prosperous growth after the Third Plenary Session of the 11th CPC Central Committee. Benefitting from political and economic development, various forms of news media advanced side by side in competitive and cooperative relationships, governed by an interlocking division of labor. Their simultaneous progression answered the needs of China's Socialist modernization, although the presence of defects pointed to the need of further reforms.

Newspapers

The expansion of China's newspaper industry after the Third Plenary Session of the 11th CPC Central Committee was manifested in several aspects:

The surge in the number of newspapers and the total circulation

According to a nationwide survey on newspapers conducted in 1985, the period of January 1, 1980 to March 1, 1985 saw birth to as many as 1,008 newspapers. In other words, a brand new newspaper hit the stand every other day. Compared with the small number of 253 — counting those distributed through the postal system — back in 1978, there were 1,618 newspapers registered for public circulation by the end of 1989. From 1978 to 1989, the number of newspapers had grown 6.4 times at an annual rate of 18.4%, with the apexes of newspaper launches being 1980, 1985, and 1987. In 1980, there were 35% more newspapers in China than in the previous year; in 1985, the rate of year-on-year increase was 32%; and from 1986 to 1987, the number of newspapers doubled. 1987 was also the year when the newly established State Press and Publication Administration conducted a new round of registration for all newspapers for the sake of improving their quality and scope of distribution. After the re-registration in 1987, the total number of newspapers in public circulation was 1,482. In 1988, the number went up steadily to 1,628, to be maintained at 1,618 in 1989.

Accompanying the increase in the number of newspapers was an expansion in total circulation. In 1978, the total circulation of newspapers delivered by post was close to 55.43 million per issue, whereas at the end of 1989, the identical figure for newspapers with a Domestic Universal Publication Number (*Quanguo tongyi kanhao* 全國統一刊號, often abbreviated as *kanhao*) hit 154.28 million, 2.75 times that of 1978. In 1986, a new height of 207.22 million was attained, meaning that one in every five persons in China owned a newspaper.

In addition to those registered for public circulation, there were thousands of newspapers published with an internal *kanhao*, circulating among smaller groups of readers, such as members of industrial enterprises. According to a survey conducted for 27 provinces, municipalities, and autonomous regions in 1989, there were 4,014 such newspapers.

The expansion of the size of workers

The expansion of the newspaper industry was also reflected in the size of newspaper workers. In 1989, editors, reporters, administrative staff, and managerial staff engaged in newspaper publication together made up a team of over 100,000, 58% larger than that of 1983. It is worth pointing out, however, that the training of journalists did not always keep pace with the surge in demand. As a result, a portion of the journalists were of dubious quality.

Diversification

The 1980s was a time of diverse development for the newspaper industry. Diversity was achieved in numerous aspects, including the newspaper categories, the languages of publication, and the financing of newspapers.

Newspaper categories

Table 23.1 shows the distribution of the 1,442 newspapers published with a universal *kanhao* issued by the State Press and Publication Administration at the end of 1990, as listed in *China Journalism Yearbook* (*Zhongguo xinwen nianjian* 中國新聞年鑑), by categories.

Table 23.1   The distribution of newspapers by categories (end of 1990)

Category	Number of newspapers	Percentage	Ranking in terms of percentage
Official CPC newspapers (Party organs)	406	28.2%	1
Economic newspapers	137	9.5%	2
Enterprise newspapers	135	9.4%	3
Industry newspapers	87	6%	4
Minority newspapers	80	5.5%	5
Science and technology newspapers	75	5.2%	6
Radio and television newspapers	55	3.8%	7
Newspapers for students, teenagers, and children	42	2.9%	8
Cultural newspapers	42	2.9%	8
Newspapers on demographics, society, and lifestyles	40	2.8%	9
Legal newspapers	39	2.7%	10
Medical and healthcare newspapers	38	2.6%	11
Evening newspapers	38	2.6%	11
Educational newspapers	28	1.9%	12
Farmers' newspapers	24	1.7%	13
Newspapers for the armed forces	22	1.5%	14
Workers' newspapers	21	1.5%	14
Youth newspapers	20	1.4%	15
Sports newspapers	20	1.4%	15
Official People's Political Consultative Conference and minor political party newspapers	18	1.2%	16
Senior newspapers	16	1.1%	17
Digest newspapers	16	1.1%	17
Book news publications	14	1%	18
Newspapers on the environment and city appearance	11	0.8%	19
Newspapers for overseas Chinese	8	0.6%	20
Foreign-language newspapers	6	0.4%	21
Women's newspapers	4	0.3%	22

In terms of the average circulation per issue, the top 12 newspaper categories in 1990 are listed in Table 23.2.

Table 23.2   The most circulated newspaper categories (end of 1990)

Category	Circulation	Ranking in terms of circulation
Radio and television newspapers	2,730	1
Official CPC newspapers	2,578	2
Newspapers for students, teenagers, and children	1,279	3
Digest newspapers	1,069	4
Economic newspapers	708	5
Evening newspapers	662	6
Political and legal newspapers	593	7
Cultural newspapers	467	8
Industry newspapers	448	9
Educational newspapers	416	10
Farmer's newspapers	379	11
Science and technology newspapers	370	12

Languages

Minority and English-language newspapers grew and flourished alongside the mainstream Chinese publications. According to *China Journalism Yearbook*, at the end of 1990, there were 80 newspapers being published in one of the 13 ethnic minority languages, 5.5% of the total number of newspapers in the country (see Table 23.3). The average circulation per issue of these minority papers was 780,000, 0.56% that of all newspapers. English-language newspapers, spearheaded by *China Daily* in 1981, were products of the Reform and Opening Up policy. At the end of 1990, six English-language newspapers were running in China, making up 4% of the total number. The average circulation per issue was 320,000, or 0.2% of the nation's total newspaper circulation.

Table 23.3   Minority-language newspapers (end of 1990)

Minority language	Number of newspapers
Mongolian	19
Uygur	19
Tibetan	14
Kazakh	9
Korean	8

(Cont'd)

Minority language	Number of newspapers
Lisu	3
Tai	2
Jingpho	1
Kyrgyz	1
Nakhi	1
Xibe	1
Yi (Nuosu)	1
Zhuang	1

Sources of finance

Economic reform gradually changed the financial sources of newspapers. The days when production was the sole business began to give way to a new era of corporate management. Many newspaper groups had broken away from their complete dependence on government subsidies, and were eager to reform internal management and embrace diverse business opportunities in order to stand on their own feet. A survey on 175 newspaper groups in 15 provinces, municipalities, and autonomous regions by the State Press and Publication Administration in 1988 showed that 95, or 54%, of them had caught up to this trend. From 1980 to 1985, 40 newspapers became self-funded entities operating on independent budgets. The business opportunities that provided newspapers with new sources of finance included:

- Advertising. Leveraging the development of the commodity economy, 92% of the newspapers in public circulation had started up their advertising business. In terms of advertising income, the newspaper industry was leader of the four major advertising media, gaining the largest share of the 2.33 billion total revenue in 1990. Advertising revenue became the largest source of income for newspapers.

- Diverse channels of circulation. By the end of 1990, 128 among the 300 official newspapers of the municipal party committees in public circulation had withdrawn from the postal circulation system and established their own circulation networks. This denoted the addition of 32 such newspapers on top of the 92 of 1989, making the total a third of all newspapers in China. Experience starting from 1985 proved such independent circulation networks not only more efficient in general and more convenient to the readers, but also effective in reducing the financial strains on local governments. However, the practice did not last long, as there were problems that required further explorations.

- Other printing businesses (for newspaper groups that had their own printing houses).
- Subsidiary newspapers or magazines. According to statistics from 1985, 125 newspaper groups had set up at least one subsidiary newspaper, and 83 owned at least one subsidiary magazine.
- Service businesses associated with the news industry. The same 1985 survey observed that 188 newspaper groups were supported by subsidiary businesses.

The formation of a new industry structure

The political, economic, scientific, technological, and cultural development promoted by the Reform and Opening Up policy was extended to the newspaper industry. As a result, its monotonic, Party-organ-dominant structure was enriched by some degree of diversity. With official Party papers remaining the pivot, the industry began to be reshaped by a multi-layer structure that was supplemented with varying types of publications. The core components of this new structure were as follows:

Official Party newspapers

The Third Plenary Session of the 11th CPC Central Committee was followed by the flourishing of official Party newspapers at all levels, which was especially eminent into the 1980s. From 1980 to 1985, 103 official Party papers were born, accounting for 28% of the total number of the same type of newspapers (367).

The centrality and leading role of official Party organs was established back in the 1950s. They were distinguished by advantages that allowed for the efficient communication of the Party's principles and policies:

- Large quantity. With a total number of 406, official Party organs constituted the largest newspaper category in 1990, accounting for 28.2% of all formally published newspapers (1,442).
- Large circulation. Official Party papers at various levels had an average circulation per issue of nearly 25.79 million in 1990, i.e., 18.4% of the total circulation (139.86 million).
- Large capacity. In the same year, 60 of the official Party papers in Chinese were broadsheets, making up 21.5% of all newspapers of this size (279). Taking those in minority languages into account would have made the proportion even more impressive.
- A large number of daily newspapers. Among China's 152 dailies in 1990, 106, or 70%, were official Party organs.

- Diversity in languages. Official Party papers were published in 13 ethnic minority languages apart from Chinese.
- Sizable and high caliber staff. Among the nation's 100,000 news workers, 64.6% worked at an official Party newspaper, and they were usually the more experienced.
- Large and extensive readership. The readership of official Party newspapers won out over that of other papers both in size and scope.

Special-subject newspapers

These included papers dedicated to a wide range of subjects, the four most popular being economics and business, science and technology, education, and the law, which reflected the CPC's emphasis on these areas in the course of Socialist modernization. Special-interest newspapers mushroomed upon the kickoff of Reform and Opening Up, and their total number had grown to 635 by June 1991.

The launch of *Economic Daily* and *Market Daily* (*Shichang bao* 市場報) set off a boom in economic newspapers, a mark of the 1980s no less prominent than the burgeoning economy. National papers covering macroeconomic policies and regulations emerged alongside regional varieties of newspapers focusing on microeconomic information, particularly channels of production and sales. Publications charged with the mission of stimulating internal economic growth were complemented by others that served the goal of economic opening. There were yet other specialized areas of interest, including news of specific industries, economic reform theories, and product or service information. Altogether, they contributed to the communication of economic and business information, the development of the commodity economy, as well as the advancement of economic reform.

Science and technology newspapers gained momentum from the 1978 National Science Conference. Those targeting rural areas took off most rapidly in the first half of the 1980s, popularizing scientific knowledge and in turn benefiting agricultural production. Many science and technology papers achieved impressive circulation figures. For example, *Hunan Science and Technology News* (*Hunan keji bao* 湖南科技報), for example, recorded an average circulation per issue of close to 1.8 million. *Shandong Science and Technology News* (*Shandong keji bao* 山東科技報) set an even higher circulation record of over 2.3 million in the same year.

Educational newspapers rose in response to the new impetus given to education development at the Third Plenary Session of the 11th CPC Central Committee. In 1983, Deng endorsed the debut of *China Education Daily* (*Zhongguo jiaoyu bao* 中國教育報), a publication of the Ministry of Education, by offering it a handwritten masthead. Soon, similar papers were set up by regional education authorities. Besides these official organs, newspapers oriented towards primary and secondary school students also sprang up across the country, providing their young readers with ideological education, supplementary educational materials, and information on extracurricular activities. At the tertiary level, among the 1,076 institutions in 1990, 800 ran a college newspaper, whose functions typically included disseminating the government's educational policy, publicizing the institute's directions, enhancing ideopolitical education, fostering education reform, and cultivating campus culture.

Legal newspapers sprouted with the consolidation of Socialist democracy and law. In 1980, *China Legal System News* (*Zhongguo fazhi bao* 中國法制報) was established, and became the only Chinese legal newspaper available for public circulation both within and without the country. Its circulation performance was soon proven. Having passed the 1 million mark in 1984, the paper soon expanded into a daily in 1986, enjoying a circulation of 1.7 million per issue. In 1987 and in 1988, when it took on its current name of *Legal Daily* (*Fazhi ribao* 法制日報), the average figure grew to over 2 million. Despite a slight slip back to 1.5 million in 1990, the *Legal Daily* was still the fourth ranked among all of China's daily newspapers. The example of the then *China Legal System News* was immediately followed in 29 provincial administrative divisions as well as some prefectures and cities. Bringing legal knowledge to the masses and fostering the development of Socialist democracy and law were the common objectives and achievements of these newspapers.

Apart from economic, science and technology, educational, and legal newspapers, other special-subject newspapers managed by the State Council's subsidiaries (including some state-owned specialized companies) also experienced a great flourishing between 1984 and 1988. By 1989, the majority of economy-related departments and companies under the umbrella of the State Council had established a newspaper for the industry or sector concerned. While concentrating on a specific sector or subject, these newspapers were directed towards the general public. Depending on their intended functions, news on culture, health care, sports, demographics, society, and lifestyles provided guidance for the associated industries as well as served the day-to-day needs of the general readership.

Newspapers for specific audiences

Some newspapers were designated for specific demographics. Target audiences could be defined by age or gender groups (such as children, young people, senior citizens, and women), occupations (such as workers, farmers, and the armed forces), and ethnicity (such as overseas Chinese, Chinese ethnic minorities, and foreigners). After the implementation of Reform and Opening Up, newspapers for specific audiences multiplied. The number reached 243 in 1990, making up 17% of the nation's 1,442 formally published newspapers. As far as circulation was concerned, the average figure per issue in 1990 was 24.81 million, around 18% of the average total, which was 139.86 million.

Newspapers for the youth, teenagers and children, and senior citizens catered to the needs of various age groups. Youth newspapers were primarily governed by the missions of cultivating solidarity, education, and guidance, as were epitomized by *China Youth Daily*, which circulated 1.38 million copies in 1990, the fifth highest among all daily newspapers. Teens and children's papers aimed at fostering their target readers' well-rounded development. Their number grew five times from 8 before the Cultural Revolution to 42 in 1990, with an average circulation per issue of 12.79 million. A favorable factor of the growth was that Reform and Opening Up had allowed for the diversification of publishers from the China Youth League to various educational authorities, the China Writers Association, the China Association for Science and Technology, and Children's Palaces.[24] There was even room for papers run by teenagers and children, such as *Little Masters Post* (*Xiao zhuren bao* 小主人報) and *A Million of Us* (*Women yibai wan* 我們一百萬) from Shanghai. The expansion had also benefited from the increase in papers devoted to specific subjects. Moreover, teens' and children's papers often organized social activities with the aim of integrating fun and education.

The development of newspapers for senior citizens in the 1980s was a sign of society's increasing concern over the aging population. At the end of 1990, there were 16 formally published senior papers, including the national *China Elderly News* (*Zhongguo laonian bao* 中國老年報) and *Chinese Elderly News* (*Zhonghua laonian bao* 中華老年報) as well as those of a regional variety, making up an average circulation per issue of 1.21 million. Their roles included publicizing the CPC's policy on the elderly, defending seniors' rights, serving senior citizens, and promoting elderly care across society.

Women's newspapers drew attention to changes in women's political status, thinking, and lifestyles during the Reform and Opening Up era. Representing the voices of women, they advocated for women's rights, promoted the spirits of self-esteem, self-confidence, self-reliance, and self-empowerment among women, and highlighted issues and phenomena that went against the interests of women and children. Another theme of women's papers was the family, which involved publishing advice concerning love, marriage, family lives, and social relationships. The pioneering example was *China Women's News* (*Zhongguo funü bao* 中國婦女報) by the All-China Women's Federation, which circulated 270,000 copies per issue on average. A few more could be found at the provincial level.

Moving onto occupation-based publications, the development of workers' newspapers, to begin with, was best demonstrated by the resumed publication of the *Workers' Daily* in 1978. In 1990, its average circulation per issue rose to 1.69 million, surpassed only by *Reference News* (3.26 million) and the *People's Daily* (3.09 million). Workers' papers were established by labor unions of most provincial administrative divisions, as well as cities with a high concentration of workers, and thus closely associated with the work of labor unions in defending labor rights. In broader terms, economic development was the dominant subject, with the greatest emphasis falling on production propaganda. Role models of workers often found coverage in workers' newspapers before other publications. Likewise, new issues in the implementation of Reform and Opening up were timely reported.

Another major category of occupation newspapers, farmers' newspapers were born out of the rural reform introduced after the Third Plenary Session of the 11th CPC Central Committee. *China Farmers' News* (*Zhongguo nongmin bao* 中國農民報) was set up as a weekly in 1980, and renamed *Farmers' Daily* (*Nongminri bao* 農民日報) in 1985 when it began six-day publication. At the provincial level, apart from farmers' newspapers, there were official Party organs issued in rural editions. The fostering of rural reform was the kernel of all farmers-oriented newspapers, which found expression in the promotion of Party rural policy and agricultural technology.

Newspapers for the armed forces comprised those reporting news on the military, the People's Armed Police, and public security. Most of them were only circulated domestically. Originally an internal publication, the *People's Liberation Army Daily* went into public circulation within and without China in 1987, and *China Police Daily* (*Renmin gong'an bao* 人民公安報) was founded as a public publication right from the beginning in 1984.

Last but not least were newspapers dedicated to overseas Chinese, the ethnic minorities, and foreign readers. Their political and economic significance went far beyond their circulations, which appeared modest when compared with those of other newspaper categories.

The national newspaper for overseas Chinese, *Asia Today* (*Hua sheng bao* 華聲報) was established in 1983. There were also regional papers based in places like Guangdong, Fujian, Guangxi, Yunnan, Shanghai, Zhejiang, and Hainan. In addition to the emigrated communities, their target readership included Chinese returnees, families of the returnees and overseas Chinese nationals, and Chinese people working overseas. Propaganda on the progress of economic development and improvements in people's livelihoods in the "native towns" was widely conducted to strengthen the bond between the overseas Chinese communities and their motherland as well as to stimulate patriotism.

Ethnic minority newspapers, then available in 13 languages, were key to the maintenance of national coherence and the prosperity of the minority regions. They will be detailed in a later part of this section.

China Daily was the only English-language newspaper established in those days. Its birth in 1981 bore witness to China's increasing openness and strengthening relationship with the outside world. Targeting foreigners in China as well as readers outside the country, it was also highly valued by the overseas Chinese. Domestic news on China's political, economic, social, and cultural development was reported in easy-to-read English, with a focus on explaining the Reform and Opening Up policy, while international news stories were direct reprints of releases by the world's major news agencies.

Service newspapers

Service newspapers, as they were called, aimed to provide services to the readers. Here, a broad definition of "service" applied: The first kind of service was information or knowledge provision, or more plainly, the provision of press digests. Examples included Xinhua's *Reference News*, the Shanghai Liberation Daily Press Group's *Press Digest* (*Baokan wenzhai* 報刊文摘), and *Guangming Daily*'s *News Digest* (*Wenzhai bao* 文摘報). The other kind of service involved the provision of leisure or entertainment information, such as radio and television, health care, and sports guides and news. Their vibrancy testified to people's diverse needs and interests in their after-work lives.

The greatest value of digest papers to the modern reader was speed. A reader could now absorb as much of the overflowing information as possible in the shortest time. *Reference News* became the most-circulated daily in 1990, printed in 3.26 million copies per day. Its daily selections of translated news reports, commentaries, and other articles from news publications and news agencies around the globe, including Hong Kong and Taiwan, were welcomed as a window to the outside world. In the arena of digests of domestic newspapers, *Press Digest*, which achieved a circulation of 2.79 million copies per issue in 1990, inspired the setting up of similar publications in Sichuan, Anhui, Fujian, and Beijing. Most of them were weekly papers that extracted domestic and international hot news items of the past week.

Radio and television newspapers, weekend newspapers, health newspapers, and sports newspapers underwent the most remarkable development among all leisure and entertainment service papers since the 1980s. Radio and television newspapers emerged one after another as television sets became familiar in Chinese households and television shows multiplied. At the time of the writing of this book, 55 radio and television newspapers create a total average circulation per issue of 27.3 million, overtaking official Party newspapers as the most popular category. To name some popular examples, in 1990, CCTV issued 1.41 million copies of its *China Television News* (*Zhongguo dianshi bao* 中國電視報) per issue, while the identical figures for *Shanghai Radio & TV Weekly* (*Meizhou guangbo dianshi* 每週廣播電視) and *Guangdong Television Weekly* (*Guangdong dianshi zhoubao* 廣東電視週報) were 2.75 million and 1.8 million, respectively. These radio and television papers not only published program forecasts, but also informative and entertaining columns with wide appeal.

The trend of weekend papers also had its beginnings in the 1980s, when several major newspapers took the lead in issuing weekend editions, although this trend only matured in the 1990s. According to a rough survey, as of May 1992, all the first-developed major national newspapers (i.e., the *People's Daily*, *People's Liberation Army Daily*, and *Economic Daily*), two-thirds of the official newspapers of provincial-level Party committees, and a third of the official newspapers of the central ministries and commissions were operating weekend papers in various forms. While being general-interest newspapers, weekend papers could be categorized as a kind of "service paper" as they fulfilled people's thirst for knowledge about pressing social issues as well as information on after-work pursuits, which explained their popularity.

Improvements in the general living standards also led to increasing health consciousness, and this in turn created a large market for informative, practical health newspapers. With an average circulation of 690,000 per issue, *Family Doctor* (*Jiating yisheng bao* 家庭醫生報) from Jiangxi was the most-circulated of its kind in 1990.

Sports newspapers took off together with the sports fervor that gripped the nation in the 1980s. In Beijing, the resumed *China Sports* (*Tiyu bao* 體育報) was expanded and renamed *China Sports Daily* (*Zhongguo tiyubao* 中國體育報) in 1988. Outside the capital, all kinds of sports papers burst forth, among which the most popular were those dedicated to a specific sport, such as Guangzhou's *Soccer News*

(*Zuqiu* 足球). Since its debut in 1979, it had maintained a stable circulation, which in 1990 was 667,000.

In addition to these categories, some less mainstream types of leisure and entertainment service papers also exhibited various degrees of growth in the 1980s. Their subjects of interest ranged from book news and calligraphy to flower appreciation, shopping guides, and family life.

Evening newspapers

Evening papers presented a panoramic picture of the multifaceted urban life, fusing ideological content with soft, informative, and entertaining components.

As of May 1992, there were 48 evening papers in China. Looking back into history, evening news was a rarity in 1958, when *Xinmin Evening News* (*Xinmin wanbao* 新民晚報) from Shanghai, *Yangcheng Evening News* (*Yangcheng wanbao* 羊城晚報) from Guangzhou, *Beijing Evening News* from the capital city, and *New Evening Post* (*Xin wanbao* 新晚報) from Tianjin were the only handful available. Although the number gradually grew to 13 in 1962, all evening newspapers were shut down during the Cultural Revolution. It was in 1980 that *Beijing Evening News*, *Yangcheng Evening News*, and *Xinmin Evening News* came back in print, and in nine years' time, the total circulation of China's evening papers added up to more than 10 million. Both *Xinmin Evening News* and *Yangcheng Evening News* exceeded the 1 million mark, the former achieving 1.84 million, while the latter 1.72 million.

Circulations of evening papers in the 1980s hit an all-time high ever since their start in China. Moreover, a breakthrough was also seen in terms of regional distribution. Evening papers were no longer large-city exclusives. Remote cities and ethnic minority regions, such as Lhasa, Ürümqi, Hohhot, Nanning, and Guiyang, as well as medium-sized and small cities that were not provincial capitals also picked up this trend of journalism. A few evening papers were even available in minority-language editions. They included *Wulumuqi Evening News* (*Wulumuqi wanbao* 烏魯木齊晚報), which had an Uygur edition, and *Lasa Evening News* (*Lasa wanbao* 拉薩晚報), which was also published in Tibetan.

Evening newspapers could be divided into three categories. The first included independent publications that had a clear "division of labor" with their morning counterparts. *Xinmin Evening News* and *Yangcheng Evening News* were some of the best examples. The second were supplements to the official dailies of provincial-level Party committees, such as *Yangtse Evening Post* (*Yangzi wanbao* 揚子晚報) from Jiangsu and *Wuhan Evening News* (*Wuhan wanbao* 武漢晚報). The third were official evening Party newspapers, which were official organs of municipal Party committees that not only came out in the evening, but also adopted the style of evening papers. Over half of the country's evening papers belonged to this category.

By their distinctive characteristics — short articles, intensive information, timeliness, and a strong service orientation — evening papers managed to find their niche in Chinese households amid fierce competition from other types of newspapers and the broadcast media, securing a unique place in the restructuring newspaper industry after the 1980s.

Enterprise newspapers

Enterprise newspapers were business publications that covered news related to enterprise production and operations as well as the work and life of frontline enterprise employees. Like the subject matter to which they were dedicated, these newspapers were necessitated by Reform and Opening Up. By the end of 1990, the number of formally registered enterprise newspapers had grown to 1,500. The majority of them were dailies, but dozens were issued three times per week. Interactions among enterprise newspapers resulted in improvements in quality. Their potential of development was assured by the advancement of Reform and Opening Up.

Minority newspapers

Minority newspapers played a positive role in the economic development of ethnic minority regions, the cultural level of these ethnic groups, as well as the general coherence of the nation. The first minority-oriented media to be developed, they also contributed to the multi-language skeleton of the structure of China's journalism.

China's ethnic-minority-language newspapers were mainly distributed in the 12 provinces or autonomous regions of Inner Mongolia, Xinjiang, Tibet, Qinghai, Sichuan, Guizhou, Yunnan, Hunan, Heilongjiang, Liaoning, and Jilin. Most minority groups that had their own writing systems had newspapers published in their languages.

Party newspapers formed the mainstream of minority newspapers. Inner Mongolia, Xinjiang, and Tibet first set the precedent of a radial hierarchical structure, where provincial-level Party papers occupied the very center, with professional, science and technology, youth, and other types of newspapers lying outside this. The mission of minority newspapers, which was in tune with the Party's principles on journalism, had been spelled out from the beginning: to serve as the mouthpiece of the Party and the people, propagate the Party line, and publicize the Party's policies on ethnic equality, religious freedom, and autonomy in minority regions.

Specifically, the development of minority newspapers after Reform and Opening Up was as follows:

Sichuan was home to the first newspaper in the Yi script, *Liangshan News* (*Liangshan bao* 涼山報), which was later renamed *Liangshan Daily* (*Liangshan ribao* 涼山日報). The Yi-script edition was established in January 1978 as an official organ of the Liangshan Yi Autonomous Prefectural Party Committee along with the existing Chinese edition. Up into the 1990s, the proportion of journalists who wrote primarily in the Yi script was on the rise, and the Yi-script edition was no longer only a translation of the Chinese edition. In April 1991, the first county-level Party committee organ in the Yi script was launched in the Ebian Yi Autonomous County, by the name of *Ebian Ethnic News* (*Ebian minzu bao* 峨邊民族報).

Xinjiang from the late 1970s onwards was a breeding ground for minority newspapers of all kinds. *Turpan News* (*Tulufan bao* 吐魯番報), the official newspaper of the Turpan Prefectural Party Committee, began formal publication in July 1, 1988 following its trial run since the beginning of the year, in Uygur and Chinese editions. The paper was characterized by its eye-catching layout, substantial columns, intense local aura, as well as vivid modern flair. Names of its characteristic columns included "Under the Flaming Mountains," Commoners of Huozhou," and "Fields of Hope." The major newspapers from this region that were available in ethnic minority languages are listed out in Table 23.4.

In Inner Mongolia, Mongolian was the dominant language of its ethnic minority newspapers. One of the most important party newspapers was *Alashan News* (*Alashan bao* 阿拉善報), which was launched simultaneously in Mongolian and Chinese by the Alxa League Party Committee in 1985. Its journalists were renowned for riding deep into the desert, which gave the publication the reputation of "the newspaper run on the back of camels." Also worth highlighting was the Hinggan League Party Committee's *Xing An Daily* (*Xing'an ribao* 興安日報), which printed its first issue in color on the National Day of 1983 since its first appearance in 1981. After that, color printing was used on every National Day and during the Chinese New Year, making *Xing An Daily* the first color-printed newspaper in Mongolian. A list of the major newspapers in Mongolian that were founded in Inner Mongolia around the 1980s can be found in Table 23.5.

In Tibet and Qinghai, the development of Tibetan newspapers outpaced papers of other minority languages. Soon after its establishment in 1987, the Xigazê Prefectural Party Committee's *Xigaze News* (*Rikaze bao* 日喀則報), the first general-interest paper in the Tibet Autonomous Region, fulfilled its stabilizing mission by denouncing separatist behavior together with other news media. Along the same line, *Lasa Evening News* by the Lhasa Prefectural Party Committee published a mission statement at its debut on July 1, 1985:

> "To be a good mouthpiece of the Party and the government, an important propaganda tool of the Party and the government in providing work instructions, facilitating the exchange of experience, as well as mobilizing and encouraging the solidarity of the peoples of Lahsa, for the sake of building Lahsa into a modernized historical city that is united across ethnicities, civilized and clean, as well as prosperous and well-off."

The major newspapers published in minority languages in Tibet and Qinghai during the 1980s can be found in Table 23.6.

The diverse ethnicity in Hunan, Guizhou, and Yunnan also found expression in newspaper publication in the 1980s. Newspapers were published in the Miao, Dong, Bouyei, Lisu, Zaiwa, and Nakhi languages. The most representative of them are shown in Table 23.7.

Finally, Korean-language newspapers enjoyed considerable development in Heilongjiang and Jilin during the 1980s, and the most important of them are displayed in Table 23.8. Among them, *Heilongjiang News* (흑룡강신문 黑龍江新聞) began as a Korean weekly, and then daily edition of the *Heilongjiang Daily* (*Heilongjiang ribao* 黑龍江日報). In January 1983, the division running the Korean edition became a standalone organization. The present name, *Heilongjiang News*, was taken in 1986, when the group was renamed the Heilongjiang News Agency.

Table 23.4 Newspapers in minority languages founded or resumed in the 1980s in Xinjiang

Newspaper	Foundation	Available language(s)	Organ(s) of publication	Remarks
Turpan News (Tulufan bao 吐鲁番报)	1988	Uygur and Chinese	Turpan Prefectural Party Committee	—
Yarkent News (Ye er qiang bao 莱尔羌讯报)	1985	Uygur and Chinese	Party Committee of the Third Agricultural Division of the Xinjiang Production and Construction Corps	Focused on propelling reform towards the ends of economic and cultural vibrancy
Bortala News (Bortala bao 博尔塔拉报)	1982 (Mongolian)	Mongolian, Uygur, and Chinese	Bortala Mongol Autonomous Prefectural Party Committee	—
Ba Yin Guo Leng Daily (Bayinguoleng ribao 巴音郭楞报)	R1985	Mongolian, Uygur, and Chinese	Bayingolin Mongol Autonomous Prefectural Party Committee	—
Nanjiang Oil News (Nanjiang shiyou bao 南疆石油报)	1985	Uygur and Chinese	Political Department of the Headquarters of the Southern Xinjiang Petroleum Exploration Society; then Party Committee of the Poskam Petroleum and Natural Gas Exploration Company under the Xinjiang Petroleum Administration Bureau	
Hami News (Hami bao 哈密报)	R1988 (Uygur)	Uygur and Chinese	Hami Prefectural Party Committee	—
Tarcheng News (Tacheng bao 塔城报)	R1976 (Kazakh)	Kazakh and Chinese	Tacheng Prefectural Party Committee	—
Xinjiang Legal News (Xinjiang fazhi bao 新疆法制报)	1982	Uygur and Chinese	Department of Justice of the Xinjiang Autonomous Region	China's first minority-language legal newspaper

(Cont'd)

Newspaper	Foundation	Available language(s)	Organ(s) of publication	Remarks
Xinjiang Science and Technology News (Xinjiang keji bao 新疆科技報)	1980 (Uygur); 1984 (Kazakh)	Kazakh, Uygur, and Chinese	Science and Technology Commission of the Xinjiang Autonomous Region	Originally Science and Technology (Kexue yu jishu 科學與技術); renamed in 1987
Hami Science and Technology News (Hami keji bao 哈密科技報)	1980	Uygur	Science and Technology Commission of Hami Prefecture	Terminated in 1988
Xinjiang Broadcasting and Television News (Xinjiang guangbo dianshi bao 新疆廣播電視報)	1981	Uygur and Chinese	Xinjiang People's Broadcasting Station and Xinjiang Television Station	China's first minority-language newspaper devoted to radio and television
Tarim Information (Talimu xinxi 塔里木信息)	1985	Uygur and Chinese	Science Information Institute and Science and Technology Development Center of Aksu Prefecture	Focused on economic information, but also covered science and technology, education, the grooming of talents, people's livelihoods, and health
Xinjiang Commercial Post (Xinjiang shangye bao 新疆商業報)	1988	Uygur and Chinese	Department of Commerce, Medicines Bureau, and Tabaco Corporation of the Xinjiang Autonomous Region, plus Bureau of Commerce of the Xinjiang Production and Construction Corps	China's first minority-language economic newspaper
Wulumuqi Evening News (Wulumuqi wanbao 烏魯木齊晚報)	1984	Uygur and Chinese	Ürümqi Municipal Party Committee	China's first minority-language evening newspaper

Note: "R" indicates the year of resumed publication.

Table 23.5   Mongolian-language newspapers founded in Inner Mongolia around the 1980s

Newspaper	Foundation	Available language(s)	Organ(s) of publication	Remarks
Alashan News (*Alashan bao* 阿拉善報)	1985	Mongolian and Chinese	Alxa League Party Committee	—
Xing An Daily (*Xing'an ribao* 興安日報)	1981 (Mongolian)	Mongolian and Chinese	Hinggan League Party Committee	—
Herdsmen News (*Mumin bao* 牧民報)	1988	Mongolian	Bairin Right Banner Party Committee and Government	—
Inner Mongolia Science and Technology News (*Neimenggu keji bao* 內蒙古科技報)	1981	Mongolian and Chinese	Inner Mongolia Association for Science and Technology	—
Chifeng Science and Technology News (*Chifeng keji bao* 赤峰科技報)	1978	Mongolian and Chinese	Chifeng Association for Science and Technology	Trial-run in 1978 as *Ju Ud Science and Technology News* (*Zhaowuda keji bao* 昭烏達科技報); renamed in 1984; an irregular publication
Science and Technology Information News (*keji xinxi bao* 科技信息報)	1979	Mongolian and Chinese	Technology Department of Ih Ju League	Originally *Ih Ju Science and Technology Information News* (*Yi kezhao keji xinxi bao* 伊克昭科技信息報); renamed in 1987

Table 23.6 Newspapers in minority languages founded in Tibet and Qinghai in the 1980s

Newspaper	Available languages	Foundation	Organ(s) of publication	Remarks
Xigaze News (*Rikaze bao* 日喀則報)	Tibetan and Chinese	1987	Xigaze Prefectural Party Committee	Tibet's first general-interest newspaper
Lasa Evening News (*Lasa wanbao* 拉薩晚報)	Tibetan and Chinese	1985	Lhasa Prefectural Party Committee	China's second and Tibet's first minority-language evening newspaper
Tibet Science and Technology News (*Xizang keji bao* 西藏科技報)	Tibetan and Chinese	1980 (Tibetan)	Tibet Science and Technology Commission and Association for Science and Technology	—
Tibet Legal News (*Xizang fazhi bao* 西藏法制報)	Tibetan and Chinese	1985	Department of Justice of the Tibet Autonomous Region	—
Tibet Youth News (*Xizang qingnian bao* 西藏青年報)	Tibetan and Chinese	1985	Tibet Regional Committee of the Communist Youth League	—
Qinghai Science and Technology Weekly (*Qinghai keji bao* 青海科技報)	Tibetan and Chinese	1984 (Tibetan)	Qinghai Association for Science and Technology	Masthead of the Tibetan edition written by Choekyi Gyaltsen, the 10th Panchen Lama
Qinghai Tibetan Legal News (*Qinghai zangwen fazhi bao* 青海藏文法制報)	Tibetan	1983	Department of Justice of Qinghai Province	Chin's first Tibetan newspaper devoted to legal education
Gangchen Teen News (*Gangjian shaonian bao* 剛堅少年報)	Tibetan	1989	Qinghai Nationalities Publishing House	China's first Tibetan teens' newspaper
Qaidam Mongolian News (*Chaidamu mengwen bao* 柴達木蒙文報)	Mongolian	1987	Haixi Mongol and Tibetan Autonomous Prefectural Party Committee	Qinghai's only newspaper in Mongolian

Table 23.7 Newspapers in minority languages founded in the 1980s in Hunan, Guizhou, and Yunnan

Newspaper	Available language(s)	Foundation	Organ(s) of publication	Remarks
Xiangxi Miao News (Xiangxi miaowen bao 湘西苗文報)	Miao	1984	Miao-Language Office under the Ethnic Affairs Commission of the Xiangxi Tujia and Miao Autonomous Prefecture	An irregular publication
Taijiang Miao News (Taif Jangb Baod Leix Amub 台江苗文報)	Miao	1986	Ethnic Affairs Commission of Taijiang County, Qiandongnan Miao and Dong Autonomous Prefecture	Most news and articles were published bilingually in the local Miao script and in Chinese
Miao and Dong News (Baod Leix Hmub Leix Gud 苗文侗文報)	Miao and Dong	1984	Ethnic Affairs Commission of the Qiandongnan Miao and Dong Autonomous Prefecture	China's only newspaper featuring two minority languages; an irregular internal publication
Bouyei News (Baoq Selqyaix 布依文報)	Bouyei	1983	Ethnic Affairs Commission of Luodian County, Qiannan Buyei and Miao Autonomous Prefecture	—
Wangmo Bouyei News (Wangmo xian buyi wen bao 望漠縣布依文報)	Bouyei	1983	Ethnic Affairs Commission of Wangmo County, Qianxinan Buyei and Miao Autonomous Prefecture	—
Nujiang News (Nujiang bao 怒江報)	Lisu and Chinese	1983	Nujiang Lisu Autonomous Prefectural Party Committee, Yunnan Province	—
Lijiang News (Lijiang bao 麗江報)	Nakhi and Lisu	1985	Ethnic Affairs Commission of the Lijiang Naxi Autonomous County, Yunnan Province	The Nakhi Edition was China's first newspaper in the language
Dehong Unity News (Dehong tuanjie bao 德宏團結報)	Tai, Jingpho, Lisu, Zaiwa, and Chinese	1985 (Zaiwa)	Dehong Dai and Jingpo Autonomous Prefectural Party Committee, Yunnan Province	China's only newspaper available in five languages, including Chinese

Table 23.8 Korean-language newspapers founded in Heilongjiang and Jilin in the 1980s

Newspaper	Foudation	Available language(s)	Organ(s) of publication	Remarks
Heilongjiang News (흑룡강신문 黑龍江新聞)	1983	Korean	Heilongjiang News Agency	A subsidiary of Heilongjiang Daily (Heilongjiang ribao 黑龍江日報) before 1983; a provincial-level Party newspaper
Jilin News (길림신문 吉林朝鮮文報)	1985	Korean	Jilin Provincial Party Committee	—
Yanbian Broadcasting and Television News (Yanbian guangbo dianshi bao 延邊廣播電視報)	1984	Korean and Chinese	Yanbian Broadcasting and Television Bureau	—
Friends of Life (Shenghuo zhi you 生活之友)	1985	Korean	Yanbian People's Broadcasting Station, Jilin Province	—

The reform of newspaper journalism

As reviewed, many positive signs were shown in the newspaper industry after Reform and Opening Up. In fact, the profound changes in newspaper journalism during this era, in aspects ranging from the contents and styles of news pieces to business operations, amounted to a reform in itself.

The restoration of news communication

The first step of reform following the Third Plenary Session of the 11th CPC Central Committee was to restore the newspaper, which had degenerated into a tool for "great criticism" during the Cultural Revolution, its primary function of news reporting. Of the expanded amount of news stories, a large proportion went to economic news, which not only promoted the government's policies regarding the economic reform, but also covered various aspects of the economic life. The scope of political, social, and world news was also widened. Special features were run for the NPC and CPPCC, accidents and disasters were brought to the surface, and sensitive international issues were discussed.

The strengthening of public voices

While positive propaganda was dominant in China's newspapers, there was some improvement in their watchdog role after Reform and Opening Up. Analytical, influential articles that reflected public opinion were published, helping the government make the right decisions. The uncovering and criticism of corruption and misconduct was also conducive to the rebuilding of Party and social morals.

Moreover, close interactions between newspaper groups and the masses were restored. To demonstrate their commitment to serving the readers, many newspapers conducted readers' surveys or hosted public cultural, sports, and philanthropic activities. It was also common practice to set apart columns or pages for letters' to the editor, allowing readers to express their criticisms and suggestions on the work of the government. The top-down approach of communications began to evolve into a two-way process that gave voice to the public.

The increase of distinctiveness

Amid the upholding of the spirit of "commonness," i.e., the adherence to the Party's principles of journalism, the absolute homogeneity of newspapers began to give way to distinctiveness. During the Cultural Revolution, the overwhelming dominance of Xinhua releases went to the very extreme: not only were they the only source of news for all newspapers; there were even uniform regulations on the placement of certain news pieces. As a result, there was very little, if any, difference between major and minor newspapers. After Reform and Opening Up, variations in the handling of Xinhua releases were observed among newspapers of different administrative levels and publication frequencies. While nationwide newspapers were most inclined to reprint Xinhua's releases, except for major news concerning the Party and the government, official organs of provincial-level Party committees could use the official releases sparingly depending on their regional relevance. Even for the national newspapers, the coverage of major news was often complemented by contributions of staff reporters. As for non-Party-committee newspapers, the adoption of Xinhua releases was not obligatory, although they might be summarized or rearranged when appropriate. This meant room for distinctiveness as much as extra space for regional or special-interest news. In the end, such diversity had the effect of stimulating reform in news agencies, prompting them to produce news that met the demand of various kinds of newspapers.

As an additional note, the appeal of special-subject newspapers often extended beyond their specific target groups and sectors of industry to the general public. As reform further progressed, regional newspapers also began to pursue local characteristics.

The increase in the depth of reporting

Reform and Opening Up was followed by two phases of change in the forms of mainstream news writing. From 1977 to 1986 was the transition from generalized reporting (which attempted to generalize trends or phenomena from a series of events) to straight news. The *People's Daily*, for example, increased the proportion of straight news from 28% to 75%, while cutting generalized news reports from 53% to 11%. The switch towards in-depth reporting took place subsequently, as readers began to probe into the "why" beyond the "what." The second transition was also necessitated by the weakening competitiveness of the newspaper as a source of news facing the rise of television. Losing out in terms of timeliness, the print media had to offer what could not be covered in broadcast hours. In-depth reporting that portrayed social changes under China's political and economic transformations on an extensive scale lent authority to newspaper journalism.

Innovations in news writing styles

With changes in the content to be reported on, as well as readers' demands brought about by Reform and Opening Up, traditional forms of news writing no longer sufficed. In their exploration for stylistic innovations, journalists came up with several novel news forms: a free-flowing form that broke away from the traditional inverted pyramid structure, a spontaneous form that resembled neither features nor prose essays, a new signed commentary style, and a comprehensive news form called "combined reporting."[25] In addition, less conventional approaches like serial journalism, investigative interviews, and eyewitness-style news features were brought into common practice, regenerating vibrancy into newspaper journalism.

The modernization of page layouts

The modernization of page layouts was most prominent in *China Daily* and the *People's Daily (Overseas Edition)*, which shouldered the role of promoting China to the outside world, as well as in the tabloids. Modern, magazine-style layouts that favored the use of large and catchy photographs rose with multicolor chromatography and color printing, and headlines were handled with unprecedentedly bold emphasis.

The revolution in page layouts could be attributed to three main factors: the influence of newspapers from overseas, Hong Kong, Macau, and Taiwan; the popularization of modern printing technologies; and relaxation in layout editing.

The adoption of modern technologies

Modern technology had a great impact on the editorial work, reporting, typesetting, printing, and circulation of the newspaper industry. The English-language *China Daily* founded in 1981 was China's first newspaper to adopt computer typesetting and offset printing. Shortly after that, the *People's Daily (Overseas Edition)* became the first Chinese-language newspaper to avail itself of not only offset printing, but also laser typesetting upon setup in 1985. Thanks to satellite transmission, the paper could be printed overseas with up-to-the-minute content. From then on, more and more newspapers started picking up laser phototypesetting and offset printing, and by the beginning of 1992, many major national newspapers and most of the official newspapers of provincial-level Party committees had adopted these technologies.[26] As a substantial number of resourceful newspapers, including some enterprise papers, turned to laser typesetting and offset printing, China's newspapers gradually bid farewell to the era of letterpress printing.

The immediate effects were improvements in speed and printing quality. Improved layouts with clear, sharp photographs were welcomed by readers, thus increasing the competitiveness of newspapers. Moreover, technology revolutionized the workflow of newspaper publication. Labor-intensiveness was reduced, errors were minimized, and efficiency surged.

The dependence on advertising income

The development of advertising businesses not only served the fast-expanding commodity economy and the readers, but also contributed to the financial independence of newspapers. Indeed, advertising income quickly grew into the largest source of finance for many newspapers.

News Agency

China's two newswires, the Xinhua News Agency and China News Service, also experienced remarkable developments following the Third Plenary Session of the 11th CPC Central Committee.

Xinhua News Agency

As China's official press agency, Xinhua proposed developing itself into a "modern Socialist international wire service with Chinese characteristics during the 1990s" in a report to the CPC Central Committee in January 1983, which was quickly endorsed by the Party.

Since then, modernization and internationalization became the central goals of Xinhua. To meet the technical level and scope of service required of an international news agency, the following objectives were laid down:

- To timely and systematically release a substantial amount of quality news reports, photography, and commentaries that covered major events and news in China as well as around the world;
- To establish a system for collecting news around the globe and develop a network of correspondents that spans all of China and most countries in the world;
- To expand and improve the system of supplying news to domestic and international newspapers, publications, radio and television broadcasters, government departments, enterprises, and other relevant users;
- To adopt the most advanced world-class communications technologies possible;
- To maintain a team of influential journalists, editors, commentators, and journalism researchers who had insights into international issues; and

- To supply economic and business news and information domestically and internationally.

Concerning its role as an official Socialist news agency, Xinhua defined "Chinese characteristics" as:

- The political characteristics of abiding by Marxism-Leninism and Mao Zedong Thought, upholding the proletarian Party spirit, propagating the Party and government's principles and policies, serving the people and Socialist modernization internally, and contributing to the promotion of international solidarity, opposition against hegemonism, striving for world peace, and fostering of progress internationally.
- The functional characteristics as the Party and government's mouthpiece. Xinhua bore the responsibilities of releasing news within and without the country as well as conducting surveys and collecting domestic and international news.
- The journalistic characteristics of supplying truthful, rigorously examined, and authoritative news, picking up on Liu Shaoqi's call for the agency's supply of "objective, truthful, fair, and comprehensive" news that "came with a stance."[27] In terms of the composition of news releases, news on China, the East, and the Third World should dominate. Moreover, Xinhua held a unique perspective over international events.

To make up for the lost time during the Cultural Revolution, Xinhua embarked on extensive research and held a series of domestic and international conferences on the principles and methods of building itself into an international news agency, based on which planning strategies were devised towards this end.

The 1980s was Xinhua's golden decade of development. The tipping point came in 1983, when the agency formally declared the goal of building itself into an international news agency and the principles of "development amid reform" and "reform amid development." Soon, these materialized in breakthroughs in its news businesses, operations management, team building, and communications technology. Its goal had been achieved by the beginning of the 1990s: the domestic-oriented news agency had evolved into a modern and sophisticated external-oriented wire service with Chinese characteristics. The changes and developments of Xinhua during this period were expressed in the following respects:

Improvements in news reporting

Regarding the reporting of domestic news, improvements were found in the composition, scope, amount, quality, and timeliness of news coverage. Concerning the selection of news in particular, both major national issues as well as local and social issues of universal significance were emphasized; practical, inspirational news was preferred above general news, while news that interested the public was favored over the pure reporting of progress in government work. Along the line of positive propaganda, achievements in the Four Modernizations and Reform and Opening Up were placed under the spotlight in order to motivate continual efforts. On the other hand, there was a strengthening of critical journalism that reflected reality, channeled public opinion, and enhanced public supervision. In the technical aspect of news writing, journalists were encouraged to write short and visual pieces in an immediate, refreshing, and friendly tone. Soon, the practices of Xinhua were dispatched along its news releases to the entire journalism industry.

To further its role in publicizing the Party's principles and policies, the official news agency devoted added effort to conducting local surveys after 1986. Journalists penetrated into society, sometimes traversing various provinces and districts, for surveys and research, yielding detailed and influential survey reports. Whether devoted to one single subject or multiple issues, and whether conducted one-off or in a series, the surveys revealed problems which had arisen since Reform and Opening Up, and provided solid bases for constructive analyses and suggestions.

To enable the timely dispatch of news all over the country, Xinhua set up major branch offices in all of China's 30 provinces, municipalities, and autonomous regions, in China and Macau, as well as smaller branches or reporting stations in some "open coastal cities" and Special Economic Zones.[28] It also had a branch office for the People's Liberation Army, and reporting stations for each military branch and major military region. With four domestic broadcasting channels, Xinhua managed to release close to 200,000 words per day. In addition, the agency supplied about 10,000 words of express releases to the big screen at the Beijing Railway Station.

Reforms were also carried out with respect to news services for international audiences as well as the coverage of world news. After a decade of effort, Xinhua expanded its text-based services into diverse ones available in six languages: Chinese, English, French, Spanish, and Arabic. In-depth stories and features on Reform and Opening Up dominated externally-oriented news releases in the 1980s, although commentaries, news analyses, and profiles were employed to add diversity. All were produced with utmost sensitivity to international opinion. Xinhua's world news leaned heavily towards Third World countries in Asia, Africa, and Latin America, which made up 60% of its world news releases. In covering the world's breaking news, the Chinese newswire exhibited the strengths of promptness, precision, and frequency during the Gulf War of 1990 to 1991: bulletins were dispatched five minutes after the outbreak of the war, and around 150 concise English releases were issued every day.

Xinhua also started releasing news photos to media and organizations around the world. In the Reform and Opening Up era, the average number of news photos released was between 28,000 and 32,000 per annum, the domestic to international ratio being roughly the same. Considering the regular users, 290 came from the Chinese Mainland, while 260 were based in other parts of the world. This urged the news agency to improve its domestic and international telegraph networks for wire photos. By the end of the 1980s, a network connecting Xinhua's headquarters and provincial branches had been established, allowing for the daily dispatch of news photos via facsimile. The construction of international telegraphs is yet underway at the time of writing, following the accomplishments of those which have reached New York, Paris, Tokyo, and Hong Kong. Alongside the building of telegraph networks, Xinhua struck photo exchange partnerships with over 30 news agencies around the world, including The Associated Press, Reuters, Agence France-Presse, and the Information Telegraph Agency of Russia, as well as business relationships with over 10 external press photo agencies.

Entrance into the world news market

From 1982 to 1992, Xinhua's overseas branches increased from 83 to over 100, overseen by the newly established Asia, Middle East, Latin America, and Africa Regional Bureaus which were based in Hong Kong, Cairo, Mexico, and Nairobi, respectively. Accordingly, the number of overseas correspondents grew from around 300 to around 500.

Before 1982, Xinhua's overseas services depended mainly on dispatch stations that received wireless broadcasts from Beijing and printed news releases locally. The inefficiency explained the low rate of usage before the switch towards telegraphy. As of 1992, its wire services benefitted 300 direct users from 58 countries and regions, which included newspapers, periodicals, radio and television broadcasters, news agencies, government departments, international organizations, and research institutes, while around 4,000 more indirect users adopted redistributed releases.

At the time of writing, Xinhua has established a round-the-clock news release system. In the normal case, an average of 250,000 words are released every day. Deducting the 110,000 from Chinese releases, 50,000 belong to Chinese-English bilingual text; 20,000 are in French, 10,000 Russian, 40,000 Spanish, and 20,000 Arabic. Economic and business news released to overseas users alone takes up 35,000 words. In addition, around 300 news features are dispatched in multiple languages to over 130 countries and regions every year. Not only are Xinhua releases welcomed by the Third World; they have also broken the monopoly of Western newswires over the world news market. By 1992, Xinhua had signed news exchange and collaborative agreements with news agencies and departments from more than 80 countries, as well as secured partnerships with Japanese and Western companies on communications technologies and photography equipment. Such expansion and development have enabled the Chinese news agency to sit among the world's six largest wire services.

The modernization of communications technology

Symbolized by the establishment of the headquarters complex, Xinhua's breakthroughs in communications technology were realized in the preliminary computerization of the transmission, editing, translation, distribution, and printing of news.

One of the achievements since modernization efforts began in the 1980s was the computerization of Chinese-language broadcasting. While shortwave facsimile broadcasting, which Xinhua had been using for domestic news distribution since the 1950s, was more advanced than the older Morse code and human decoding, its disadvantages of slow transmission speed, unclear print, and climatic or geographical disturbances left a lot to be desired. In 1985, Xinhua started introducing microcomputer local area networking (LAN) and remote data transmission technologies for newspaper offices and radio stations all over the country. By the end of 1989, this had resulted in a Chinese-language microcomputer communications network comprising four domestic computerized storage and relay systems and 103 national- and provincial-level remote receiving stations. At the headquarters, the input, proof-reading, and transmission of news had all been performed by the computer. Direct reception of Chinese text via microcomputers had raised the transmission speed by 15 times, from 2 words per seconds to 30 words per seconds. Moreover, the improved quality of the received text implied less hassle for newspapers adopting it, and hence better control of publication times.

Another progress was the gradual computerization of foreign-language news production and distribution. Over the years, writing at the typewriter, editing on paper, and distributing releases manually had characterized the daily routine of

Xinhua's foreign-language news distribution. With the installation of a computer editing and processing system for English-language news in 1986, inputting and editing could be conveniently done at the screen of computer terminals, after which the completed releases were directly dispatched by telex. The initial success was followed by the development of similar systems for news production in other languages.

Third was the computer processing of news photos. In 1986, Xinhua brought in advanced photo processing technology of the time from foreign countries, which began trial operations the next January. The reception, storage, editing, and distribution of news photos were thus computerized. The year 1987 also saw the first time when news photos were transmitted via the above-mentioned Chinese microcomputer communications network, which paved the way for the simultaneous distribution of text and photo releases.

Fourth was the adoption of portable computer news distribution systems for the coverage of important events. First made available for English-language news, the portable system debuted at the 1986 Asian Games in Seoul, followed by appearances at the Fifth Plenary Session of the Sixth NPC, the 13th CPC National Congress, and the Sixth National Games in 1987. In 1988, it was mature enough for news in Chinese and Spanish. Journalists produced news on portable computers and sent them to news distribution centers via telephone lines for editors' fine-tuning and approval at computer terminals. Finally, news was promptly released through remote transmission circuits connected to the headquarters' computer system.

Fifth, Xinhua contributed to the birth of a digital satellite live broadcasting network in China. After extensive research and experiments, it successfully adapted the satellite broadcasting equipment from an American company for *Luoyang Daily* (*Luoyang ribao* 洛陽日報) in Henan in July 1988, building China's first small digital satellite receiving station. By the end of 1991, the news agency had installed the same set of equipment for 130 prefectural newspaper groups. Satellite broadcasting proved to be the answer to the long-standing problem of the poor reception of Xinhua releases in remote areas and ethnic minority regions, as well as a direct means of distributing economic and technological information to users.

Sixth, Xinhua's communications networks were expanding and improving in quality. Domestically, microwave circuits, power cables, and satellite telephone channels knitted an exclusive network that stretched out from Beijing to 30 province-level branches and six sub-branches in 1989, enabling telephone communications and text and image facsimile. Internationally, the Beijing-center network had 53 communications circuits in the early 1990s, among which 5 were satellite telephone channels (between Beijing and Hong Kong, Paris, New York, Tokyo, and Moscow, respectively) and 48 were telegraph channels, passing through a total of 49 countries and regions.[29] In fact, Xinhua's relay stations in Paris, London, New York, and Hong Kong were already functioning with computer-controlled automatic telegraph switching systems back in 1978. These systems were connected to the headquarters' foreign-language computer system, so that low-speed networking allowed for the transmission of news from stations outside China to nearby regions.

The second last achievement concerned the building of information retrieval systems. Xinhua's *News Thesaurus* (*Xinwen xu ci biao* 新聞敘詞表) and trial news information retrieval system passed government approval in 1987 and 1989, respectively, giving the news agency the potential to be the largest news information retrieval center in the country.

The last point goes back to Xinhua's headquarters complex, which went into operation after its formal completion in 1990. In the heart of this 28-story building, which rose 117 meters above the ground and occupied a floor area exceeding 50,000 square meters, housed a news communications project engineered from the latest computer and communications technologies. It marked the fruition of a stand-alone modern news transmission system that automated the workflow of news production, a technical prerequisite for an international news agency.

Business expansion

Reform and Opening Up brought a great turn to Xinhua's operations management. The establishment of the General Manager's Office in 1980 marked the onset of business expansion and financial reform. In 1985, the Office was renamed the Business Development Bureau, aptly manifesting its role in business development and operations management. The chief principle of business expansion was that businesses must be related to the news industry. In addition, they must also adhere to the policies and regulations of the Party and the government, bring social and economic benefits, play a part in the building of Socialist material and spiritual civilization, and serve the purpose of news propaganda.

Seeking to consolidate the twin developments of news reporting and business undertakings, Xinhua convened a meeting on the development of information services and operations management in 1988. The meeting also discussed the scope and focus of business development outside China. Other than the core work of foreign-language news distribution, proposed businesses included:

information services; the supply of news photos, features, and special dispatches; the circulation of Xinhua publications through collaboration with foreign partners; and consultation and public relations services.

Eventually, proposals and plans led to rewarding businesses. The news agency expanded into a publisher with its own newspapers and periodicals, and ran a Media Development Corporation. Its branch offices also opened new markets by setting up subsidiary news photo agencies and other media-, publication-, and culture-related economic entities. In time, the steadily-increasing profits of these businesses relieved the financial burden on the state and facilitated the healthy development of the news agency.

At the time of writing, Xinhua's 600-member management team oversees a wide range of businesses. The list includes newspaper and periodical publication, general publication, printing, photo and information services, advertising, public relations, and the development of communications technologies.

The diversification of public services

Looking at Xinhua as a public service provider, business expansion after Reform and Opening Up essentially transformed it from a unitary news distribution agency into a multifaceted news propaganda apparatus. Xinhua's news and information services were characterized by three attributes: multiple levels, multiple channels, and multiple functions.

Observing the intensifying competition among various media channels with the opening up of news sources following the Third Plenary Session of the 11th CPC Central Committee, Xinhua switched to a multi-level approach of news distribution. It divided the domestic market into four tiers: first, national newspapers; second, provincial- and county-level newspapers; third, prefectural-level newspapers (i.e., the so-called "local broadcasting"); and fourth, all radio and television broadcasters. In addition, Xinhua also developed regional news distribution services as well as supplied features or special dispatches suited to the diverse needs of newspapers and broadcasters. Except for news on sensitive issues of wide-reaching significance, regional branch offices were given the discretion to distribute special releases to local news units. Moreover, there was an increase in the domestic distribution of world news and features. Special columns and topical programs were set up for certain newspapers, radio stations, and television stations. In 1985, the increase reached the tier of prefectural-level newspapers.

By multiple channels, it meant that Xinhua devoted resources to services other than supplying news to news units, for the sake of direct news propaganda and information dissemination. The first direction was to run its own newspapers and periodicals. During the 1980s and early 1990s, Xinhua founded over 50 publications on top of the existing *Reference News*, catering to diverse target audiences. The most prominent examples are displayed in Table 23.9.

Table 23.9 Newspapers and periodicals run by the Xinhua News Agency in the late 1980s and early 1990s

Newspaper/periodical	Publication frequency
Economic Information Daily (*Jingji cankao bao* 經濟參考報)	Daily
Xinhua Daily Telegraph (*Xinhua mei ri dianxin* 新華每日電訊)	Daily
China Securities Journal (*Zhongguo zhengquan bao* 中國證券報)	Daily
Outlook Weekly (*Liaowang* 瞭望)	Weekly
Photo World (*Zhongguo tupian bao* 中國圖片報)	Weekly
China Comment (*Ban yue tan* 半月談)	Bi-weekly
Globe (*Huanqiu* 環球)	Monthly
Chinese Journalist (*Zhongguo jizhe* 中國記者)	Monthly
Photography World (*Sheying shijie* 攝影世界)	Monthly
Great Rural World (*Nongcun da shijie* 農村大世界)	Monthly
New China Quarterly*	Quarterly
China Yearbook (*Zhongguo nianjian* 中國年鑒)	Annual

* An English publication.

Second, Xinhua set out planning for the delivery of express news on public big screens in 1985. The first big screen was erected east of the Beijing Railway Station in 1988. With a space of 40 square meters, it alerted travelers and passers-by with sharp text and images and the latest top stories, as well as served as an effective propaganda channel.

Multiple functions referred to those functions apart from supplying news that served the Four Modernizations and society as a whole, as performed by Xinhua's diverse undertakings. The Xinhua Publishing House set up in 1979 specialized in topics on journalism, current affairs, and politics, publishing 250 new titles per year with a total circulation of over 500. The China Media Development Corporation established in 1984 was founded as a parent company to a number of subsidiaries including the China Global Advertising Company, China Global Public Relations Company, and Global Micrographics Company, as well as joint ventures such as the Shenzhen Media and Cultural Center, Global (Shekou) Printing Company, Hua Xin Platemaking Company, and Huayi Packaging Company. As the names of these companies reveal, their services ranged from advertising and public relations to communications technologies, photography, printing, micrographics, and translation. By the end of the 1980s, the China Media Development Corporation had become a giant enterprise group with more than 20 regional and specialized companies, ready to expand abroad. In the 1990s, the group landed in Hong Kong, Tokyo, and New York.

Attention must be given to Xinhua's information services, which the news agency started developing with its extensive information sources at home and abroad towards the end of the 1970s. Some information providers that so emerged under the umbrella of Xinhua were the China International Information Center, the China Economic Information Center, and China News Information Service. To better manage its information businesses, Xinhua set up an Economic Information Editorial Department (better known as China Economic Information Service) in 1988, overseeing the daily distribution of 200 releases by all the subsidiary companies. Substantially, Xinhua's economic information services were provided in four lines:

- The publication of *Xinhua Economic Information* (*Xinhua she jingji xinxi* 新華社經濟資訊), a three-day-a-week domestic magazine with approximately 30,000 subscribers;
- The distribution of China economic information to international clients, first in English, and then bilingually in Chinese and English, forming a clientele from Northern America, Western Europe, Japan, Southeast Asia, and Taiwan;
- The supply of professional information to tens of thousands of users from varying sectors; and
- The provision of consultation services.

As a last note, Xinhua employed a staff of 7,000 in and outside China as of 1992, including 2,000 reporters and news editors. Its Beijing headquarters had seven main editorial departments under the Editor-in-Chief's Office, namely, the Domestic News Editorial Department, International News Editorial Department, Domestic News for Overseas Service Department, News Photography Editorial Department, Sports News Editorial Department, Economic Information Editorial Department, and Reference News Editorial Department. Other major divisions of the time included the Communications Technology Bureau, Business Development Bureau, News Research Institute, Chinese Academy of Journalism, China Photo Service, China Photo Archives, Xinhua Publishing House, and a printing house.

China News Service

China News Service was reinstated in 1978, after being disestablished during the

Cultural Revolution (when all services were stopped except for the department broadcasting oral news releases, which was incorporated into Xinhua). Targeting overseas Chinese citizens, foreign citizens of Chinese origin, and residents of Hong Kong, Macau, and Taiwan, it rose to the opportunities laid out by Reform and Opening Up, introducing China's new achievements on top of promoting its diplomatic policies and policies on overseas Chinese affairs as well as traditional culture and picturesque scenery.

The reestablished China News Service had more than 400 employees. Employees in China staffed the Editor-in-Chief's Office, Domestic News Department, Hong Kong and Taiwan Department, Special Dispatch Department, Sports Department, Research Department, and Audio-Visual Movie Department of the head office, five branches in Guangdong, Fujian, Shanghai, Guangxi, and Hainan, and 12 province-level reporting stations. Outside the Chinese Mainland, it had branches in Hong Kong, Washington, Paris, Tokyo, and Sydney, a reporting station in Macau, and news distribution agencies in New York, Bangkok, and Manila. With a telegraph network built along the junctures of Beijing, New York, and Hong Kong, it managed to seal deals with 170 overseas Chinese-language newspapers, magazines, radio broadcasters, and television operators, supplying them with news releases, special dispatches, photos, news information, audio-visual materials, movies, and other news products.

In terms of the quantity of news releases, China News Service dispatched around 30 news releases of a total of approximately 15,000 words per day, issued the publication *China News* (*Zhongguo xinwen* 中國新聞) in Beijing and Hong Kong six days a week, and published the bi-monthly *China News Overseas* (*Duiwai baodao* 對外報導). Moreover, on a monthly basis, it released about 300 special dispatches, column articles, and supplement articles of a total of approximately 300,000 words, compiled a selection of around 50 journalistic articles from Mainland publications for Chinese-language newspapers and periodicals outside China, and distributed 500 news photos, some via facsimile. Speaking of photography, China News Service also supplied color photos to picture magazines, and published exhibition photos and photo albums.

Radio

Concluding the lessons from the nation's experience in radio broadcasting over the prior three decades, the 10th National Broadcasting Work Conference in October 1980 stressed the necessity of adhering to the following principles:

- Developing a correct understanding of the nature of radio broadcasting, which would manifest the Party and the government's principles and policies;
- Keeping to the correct ideological line;
- Understanding the characteristics of radio broadcasting so as to exploit its strengths and bypass its weaknesses; and
- The complementation between national and local broadcasting as well as wireless and cable radio.

Shortly after the Secretariat of the CPC Central Committee acknowledged that radio and television were the most powerful modern tools for educating the masses about Socialist civilization in 1981, the State Council took the momentous step of strengthening the Party's leadership over the two media: it replaced the Central Broadcasting Bureau with the Ministry of Radio and Television in May 1982, which took over the responsibility of convening the 11th National Radio and Television Work Conference in March and April 1983.

The conference made concrete proposals for reforming radio and television broadcasting. In the respect of news reporting, radio and television broadcasters were urged to optimize timeliness, provide planned and continuous coverage of major events, make good use of recorded reporting, live reporting, and programs hosted by a presenter, adopt colloquial language, and improve the quality of news commentary by grooming new talents and inviting guests from various social sectors to appear in news shows. In the reform of radio and television programs, newscasts should be a top priority. In the technical aspect, the conference gave the green light to the setting up of radio and television stations at all four levels of administrative divisions, which allowed for the mixed coverage of national and local broadcasting services. It also gave momentum to the launching of broadcast satellites and the building of receiving and relay stations, the development of microwave circuits for television broadcasting alongside FM and medium-wave broadcasting, the improvement of rural broadcasting networks, the strengthening of the transmitter power output (TPO) of external broadcasting, and the enhancement of television broadcasting equipment in the border, coastal, and ethnic minority regions.

A grand vision was set forth: China was to establish a Socialist modernized radio and television network with Chinese characteristics, which integrated wireless and cable technologies, operated at the national and regional levels across urban and rural areas, and catered to domestic as well as international audiences. Within three to five years, all of China except the sparsely populated remote areas was to be covered by radio signals, and most counties were to be equipped with television reception. Towards the end of the century, television was to enter every household with the launching of television satellites. The radio and television network would provide news, information, knowledge, art and literature content, and entertainment that served the Party and the government and interested the public. Broadcasting for international audiences would be developed into 45 to 50 languages, and the total TPO would double, so that the voices of China could be heard clearly in every corner of the world.

On October 26, 1983, the CPC Central Committee endorsed the *Outline of the Report Concerning Radio and Television Work* (*Guanyu guangbo dianshi gongzuo de huibao tigang* 關於廣播電視工作的彙報提綱) submitted by the Party Leadership Group of the Ministry of Radio and Television, which asked Party committees of all levels to strengthen and improve their leadership over the two media. Other than restating the 1981 position regarding the missions of radio and television, the outline highlighted the role of technological advancement in reinforcing propaganda and patriotic education.

By the end of 1988, 461 radio stations had been established, running a total of 568 programs. The daily total broadcasting hours were 4,968, and the first programs by the national and the provincial radio stations altogether reached 70.6% of the national population. In rural areas, there were 2,521 cable radio stations, broadcasting for 65 hours in total for 7,976 households (penetration rate: 40.1%) every day. The whole country had a total of 26,197 radios, meaning an average ownership of 23.9 per 100 persons. The following sections will look at the specific achievements of China's national, local, and external radio broadcasting services after Reform and Opening Up.

The Central People's Broadcasting Station

The Central People's Broadcasting Station reformed itself along the Party line put forwards since the Third Plenary Session of the 11th CPC Central Committee. Its programs demonstrated the following improvements:

The improved focus of theoretical education

This initiative was kicked off by the hosting of the talk "The Question of Theory and Practice: Practice is the Sole Criterion for Testing Truth" in November 1978, the first of its kind in China. During 1979 and 1980, the prime time of discussion of ideological and theoretical questions, the Central People's Broadcasting Station broadcast a total of 15 talks, and from 1982 to 1983, it aired 34 more. Among the most influential were talks on "Upholding the Four Cardinal Principles," "Learning about 'On the Various Historical Issues since the Founding of the People's Republic of China,'" and "Agricultural and Economic Problems."

The increase of economic shows

The publicity of the government's economic principles and policies, regional achievements in economic development, experiences of pioneering role models, and scientific and technological innovations took up a sizable portion of the Central People's Broadcasting Station's shows. In 1983, the broadcaster launched *Mass Economy* (*Dazhong jingji* 大眾經濟), which looked into varying economic issues of wide social concern, ranging from the macro topics of business and enterprise reform and urban-rural economic revival, to the everyday problems of food, clothing, and shelter. *Broadcast to Rural Areas* (*Dui nongcun guangbo* 對農村廣播) was resumed in 1977, introducing rural reform prototypes. Also serving rural areas and agriculture were *Topics on Agricultural Science and Technology* (*Nongye kexue jishu zhuanti* 農業科學技術專題) and *Central Agricultural Broadcast and Television School* (*Zhongyang nongye guangbo dianshi xuexiao* 中央農業廣播電視學校), the latter of which gave birth to distance-learning branch schools in all provincial administrative divisions (except Tibet) and 2,270 county-level regions, as well as classes in 24,000 towns and townships. Altogether, they had recruited 830,000 registered students by the end of 1984, becoming China's largest middle-ranked technical school. The figure had yet to include the unregistered active listeners.

The enhancement of current affairs commentaries

While the Central People's Broadcasting Station did run commentary programs in the 1950s, they were strongly dependent on sources from newspapers and news agencies. There was no awareness of the significance of radio commentaries; nor was there effort in grooming an in-house commentary team. In 1980, such a team finally came into being, and the radio station's editorial departments started producing their own commentaries. Among the 132 pieces broadcast during the year, "A Heartening Trial," which went on air on September 28 criticizing the Gang of Four, was reprinted in newspapers and adopted by two foreign wire services. Between 1979 and 1984, the Central People's Broadcasting Station broadcast 800 commentaries in total.

The respect for the truth in the reporting of model stories

Attention was given to the principle of truthfulness in the reporting of model stories. Specifically, four guidelines were provided: first, the emphasis on positive reporting and commendation, complemented with appropriate criticism of negative trends; second, the conducting of in-depth investigations to obtain truthful, objective, and accurate accounts of a story, restrained by the responsibility of correction and self-criticism in the case of misrepresentation; third, the understanding of the major policy goals in each period in order to pinpoint the focus of propaganda; and fourth, the collaboration with the leadership and related government departments, with the boldness to criticize when there was a difference of opinion, given that it was faithful to the truth and the general policy.

An instance of successful coverage of role models featured meteorologist Lei Yushun, who died of cancer at the age of 48 in February 1983. In his final days, the Central People's Broadcasting Station aired a long feature titled "Middle-Aged Scientist Lei Gave His Heart and Blood for Scientific and Technological Modernization" in *Simulcast* (*Quanguo lianbo* 全國聯播) and *News and Newspaper Digest*. For a month and a half starting from January 12, more features, news stories, commentaries, letters from the audience, and recordings of Lei's last words on the sick bed could be heard continuously. The serial coverage won broadcaster prizes in the National Outstanding Radio Show Awards and National Outstanding Journalism Awards in the year of broadcast.

As far as the critical elements were concerned, an example of truthful critical reporting by the Central People's Broadcasting Station has been given in an earlier section of the chapter. [30] Another piece of award-winning serial coverage could be found in mid-1984, also broadcast in *Simulcast*. It exposed the shirking of responsibilities that led to the decade-long procrastination of the expansion of the Jilin North Railway Station. Criticism was first expressed in a letter co-written by journalists of the radio station and the *Jilin Daily* (*Jilin ribao* 吉林日報), which was followed by a series of news pieces, commentaries, recordings of telephone conversations between reporters and the radio station's editorial department, and the reading of commentators' articles over 10 days. The issue was resolved on the fourth day after the first broadcast.

The reintroduction of popular shows

Suspended during the Cultural Revolution, programs that traditionally enjoyed broad appeal, including news, educational, and service shows were gradually resumed in the 1980s.

Targeting minor citizens were *Little Trumpet* (*Xiao laba* 小喇叭) for preschoolers and *Star Torch* (*Xingxing huoju* 星星火炬) for children and teenagers. When the radio station's Children's Radio Drama Company celebrated its 30th birthday, it was honored by the inscription of Deng Xiaoping, and then the presence of Deng Yingchao, Zhou Enlai's wife and Chairwoman of the Chinese People's Political Consultative Conference, at the celebration event. For young people, the long-standing *Broadcast to the Youth* (*Dui qingnian guangbo* 對青年廣播) was renamed *Youngsters' Friend* (*Qingnian zhi you* 青年之友) in 1981. Its major missions included publicizing role models and prototypical stories, building character and morality, introducing Chinese history, educating listeners about the Party's revolutionary traditions, and providing ideas for after-school and after-work lives.

General educational programs were reformed or developed to suit the needs of the times. To give some examples, *Health Talk* (*Jiang weisheng* 講衛生) offered easy-to-understand health knowledge to the masses. Re-launched in 1978, *Around the Motherland* (*Zuguo gedi* 祖國各地) introduced new developments in various parts of China, the economic and cultural lives of various ethnic groups, as well as the geography and history of revolutionary memorial sites, scenic spots, and monuments. The show gained such popularity that some of its special features, such as "10,000 Miles down the Yangtze" and "The New Song of Yellow River," were compiled into printed books. At the end of the same year, an outward-looking counterpart was introduced with the name *Around the World* (*Shijie gedi* 世界各地), blending news, commentary, and knowledge produced from the firsthand experience of reporters traversing the world's five continents. *Sunday English Broadcast* (*Xingqiri guangbo yingyu* 星期日廣播英語) beginning in 1981 was a timely response to the new demand for English learning.

The various "audience's mailbox" shows springing up in the 1980s belonged to the category of "service programs." They included the more general *Audience Mailbox* (*Tingzhong xinxiang* 聽眾信箱) as well as those dedicated to specific subjects, such as *Farmers' Mailbox* (*Nongmin xinxiang* 農民信箱), *Sports Mailbox* (*Tiyu xinxiang* 體育信箱), and *International Issues Mailbox* (*Guoji wenti xinxiang* 國際問題信箱). Another important service program was *Advertisements* (*Guanggao* 廣告), which offered shopping guides that served the commodity economy after 1980.

Other popular programs that emerged in this period included the news and talk show *Half An Hour of Noon* (*Wujian ban xiaoshi* 午間半小時) and the music and art show *Tonight at Eight* (*Jin wan ba dian ban* 今晚八點半).

The increase of programs for ethnic minorities and Taiwan

After 1977, a series of speeches explicating the government's ethnic minority policies were broadcast, and such programs as *Ethnic Brothers* (*Xiongdi minzu* 兄弟民族) and *Great Motherland* (*Weida zuguo* 偉大祖國) appeared on the schedule of the Central People's Broadcasting Station. Reporters often traveled to minority regions to gather materials for audio news stories, and they also dug up abundant treasures for ethnic music and literature shows. In August 1982, the broadcaster collaborated with the Ministry of Radio and Television and the State Ethnic Affairs Commission in organizing an ethnic essay competition, collecting a total of 4,000 works that glorified unity across ethnic groups over a year. The outstanding works were broadcast in 1983 in the new program *Family of Nationalities* (*Minzu da jiating* 民族大家庭), and then published in the essay collection *Unity* (*Tongxin ji* 同心集). In late 1984, the Central People's Broadcasting Station decided to concentrate its efforts in producing minority-language newscasts, which included special news features and art and literature news.

Initiatives in broadcasting for Taiwan were stimulated by the NPC Standing Committee's *Message to Taiwan Compatriots* (*Gao taiwan tongbao shu* 告臺灣同胞書) of January 1979, which enunciated the principle of peaceful unification. To appeal to its target audience, the Central People's Broadcasting Station abandoned cold newspaper-style reporting in favor of friendly talk shows. In 1982, it added one more show for the Taiwanese, pushing up the total Taiwan-oriented broadcasting hours to nearly 40.

The increase of art and literature shows

Art and literature shows flourished in great diversity. Among them, music shows took up half of the broadcasting time, as an FM show was launched in mid-1980 and made available for stereo broadcasting later that year. In the same year, a policy change was made with the Chinese opera shows, which sought a concentration in the five genres of Peking opera, Pingju, Yu opera, Yueju, and Huangmei opera. Regarding literature, there were literature shows that recommended writers and literary works, explained literary basics, and reported news of the literary scene, as well as programs of novel adaptations. At the same time, radio dramas prospered with as many as 30 new series airing per year. The Central People's Broadcasting Station even cohosted a conference with the *China Theatre Association* at the end of 1980, which gave birth to the Radio Drama Society of China and three Outstanding Radio Drama Months. Furthermore, the audio editing of films and stage plays had matured. In terms of popularity, *Audio Movie Excerpts* (*Dianying luyin jianji* 電影錄音剪輯) was only second to *News and Newspaper Digest* according to the Central People's Broadcasting Station's nationwide survey in 1982.

The 1986 reform

Further reform was announced in 1986. Four program categories were identified for expansion: news, special subjects, art and literature, and service. In program development, topics relevant to listeners' lives were key. In terms of the overall programming, the radio station not only trimmed internal redundancies, but also paid attention to the division of labor with local broadcasters in order to avoid overlaps. Moreover, the prime hours in the morning, at noon, and in the evening were assigned news, integrated, and art and literature programs, respectively, according to the audience's listening behavior.

Regional radio

In the same period, parallel reform was achieved in radio broadcasting at the local levels:

The resumption and introduction of programs on ideological education

Many local radio stations resumed or launched programs for disseminating basic Marxist ideologies, which were often supplemented with the organization of public talks such as "Learning about Political Economy" and "Learning about *On Practice* (*Shijian lun* 實踐論)."

The increase of commentary

Some radio stations had regular commentary programs or program segments, under such names as "The Station's Commentary," "Short Commentary," and "One-Minute Forum," which were typically short and dedicated to a single issue. Some would invite experts, scholars, Party cadres, and government officials as guest speakers, or have their own reporters express on-the-spot comments apart from reporting.

The shift of focus in news programs to Socialist modernization

Around 50% to 60% of the news shows of local radio stations were devoted to economic development. To appeal to the masses, the flaunting of dry figures and high-sounding jargon was minimized, while practical stories on government policies, domestic and international economic conditions, as well as pioneers in economic development were frequently covered. With the onset of the rural economic reform, progress in the implementation of the household responsibility system ascended to the top of the news agenda.

The reform of freshness and timeliness

News reporting and production was intensified, so that stories of "not long ago" and "recently" became news of yesterday and today, if not dispatches of the "just happened" and "happening." Some broadcasters managed to maintain up-to-date news bulletins at mid-day as well as in the early and late evening. News items were kept short but fresh and plentiful, which in turned enriched the content of newscasts in general.

The diversification of program types

As with the national radio station, trite programs were diversified with news, educational, entertainment, and service elements at the local levels. Rural-oriented programs were the highlights of provincial radio stations; radio stations of the cities embraced the roles as farmers' "science advisors" and "leaders to prosperity." Popular science shows were given such emphasis that a special national industry seminar was called in November 1984. As of the same year, 23 radio stations in China had programs directed towards the youth, with several allotting segments of some general shows for the youngsters. *Broadcast to the Youth*, *Soul Mate of the Youth* (*Qingnian zhiyin* 青年知音), and *Contemporary Youth* (*Dangdai qingnian* 當代青年) were common names of such radio shows. Moreover, there were factual programs on history, geography, culture, and everyday knowledge; educational and entertaining talk shows, chat, and beginners' guides; and interactive programs for the exchange of ideas and questions and answers. Many radio stations also held talks on foreign languages, including English, Japanese, French, and German.

The proliferation of economic and music radio stations

The proliferating economic and music radio stations were novelties of the New Era. Among them, Guangdong's Zhujiang Economic Radio, which started operating in December 1986, was characterized by its abundance of information, its two-to-three hour programming blocks, the dominance of live shows, the all-time presence of the radio host, and the participation of the audience. It was common for hosts to read letters from the audience, receive song requests, and broadcast listeners' questions, commentaries, and opinions. After its debut, Zhujiang Economic Radio quickly became a fad in the Pearl River Delta region and along the coast of Guangdong.

The development of cable radio

Rural reform smoothed the way for the entrance of cable radio into rural areas. In its *Several Opinions on the Modification, Consolidation, and Enhancement of the Rural Cable Radio Network (Zhengdun, gonggu, tigao nongcun youxian guangbo wang de ji dian yijian* 整頓、鞏固、提高農村有線廣播網的幾點意見) in 1978, the Central Broadcasting Bureau set forth the goals of improving the service quality and technology of rural broadcasting. Henceforth, many industrial and mining enterprises, state organs, schools, bus stations, piers, train compartments, and ferries were equipped with cable radio facilities that transmitted programs from radio stations as well as broadcast tailor-made programs for their specific target audiences.

The development of programs for ethnic minorities, Taiwan, and overseas countries

In the minority provinces and regions of Xinjiang, Inner Mongolia, Tibet, Yunnan, Qinghai, and Yanbian, 24 radio stations began broadcasting in 15 ethnic languages. Broadcasting for Taiwan by local radio stations became more focused in targeting, more vibrant in content, and more innovative in format.

China Radio International

Originally part of the Central People's Broadcasting Station, the externally-oriented Radio Peking was renamed China Radio International (CRI) in 1978, with the call sign being Radio Beijing. Its programs were broadcast hourly or half-hourly, and were formulated along the four categories of news, knowledge, art and literature, and service. In addition to covering domestic and global affairs, the station shouldered the responsibility of publicizing China's recent achievements and introducing the nation's history, geography, and culture to the world. On the People's Republic of China's 35th birthday in 1981, it hosted the first live broadcast of the Tiananmen National Day celebration in English, which was simulcast through local radio stations of major cities including Beijing, Shanghai, and Guangzhou for foreigners in China. In fact, China Radio International also transmitted or sent some of its programs to broadcasters of dozens of countries on a regular basis.

Positive reception of the reformed China Radio International was soon proven by international audience polls and competitions. In America, it was selected by the readers of the Association of North American Radio Clubs' World Broadcasting Magazine as the most improved radio station in 1979. In Europe, the German Short

Wave Listeners Club Saar and Deutsche Welle named China Radio International the fifth most popular German-language broadcaster from a foreign country among 27 others in 1982. Back in Asia, a poll titled "Your Favorite Broadcast to Japan" by the Japanese radio magazine *Shortwave Monthly* (*Gekkan tanpa* 月刊短波) found CRI's Japanese programs the fourth most popular in 1982, and in 1983, the China-owned broadcaster moved up to the second rank.

Television

The development of television, especially television news, prospered in the wind of Reform and Opening Up. A decade after 1978, television ascended to be the most influential mass medium. By the end of 1989, China had developed 469 television stations and 12,658 satellite reception stations. The total number of television sets in the country had grown to 16,593, meaning that for every 100 people, 14.9 televisions were owned, which equaled a national coverage of 77.9%. According to national statistics from 1987, more than 0.6 billion people had a television at home. The following section will focus on the development of television news shows, concluding with a brief survey of other television programs.

Origins

The origins of television in China date back to 1958. However, for two decades, further progress of development was held up by material and technological constraints. Television news programs, developed for propaganda, were uniform in content and monotonous in methods of presentation. State leaders' public and diplomatic activities, and their experience and achievements in the building of Socialism were the primary content; the reading of news releases, news photo clips with voiceovers, and television newsreels were the major, if not only, forms of broadcasts.

In fact, it was television newsreels that truly dominated television programming, as the two other forms fluctuated in quantity, rendering the pre-1978 days the "newsreel era." Television newsreels had little difference from their cinema counterparts, although they were recorded on 16 mm films, which were initially in the silent black-and-white format and required the addition of real-time voiceovers, sound effects, and music. In 1963, Peking Television, the forerunner of CCTV, was equipped with the technology for producing sound movies, which was mainly used for newsreels. During the Cultural Revolution, all newsreels were embedded with pre-recorded voiceovers, sound effects, and backing music in order to eliminate uncertainties. After 1973, color film stocks gradually replaced monochrome ones, and color video recorders began to be taken up by television broadcasters. By the mid-1980s, the national and provincial-level television stations had basically familiarized themselves with the technology.

China Central Television (CCTV): the pioneer of modernization

The late 1970s marked the beginning of the modernization of television in China, and this was symbolized by the renaming of Peking Television to China Central Television (CCTV) in May 1, 1978. From then on, the television operator was equipped with electronic news-gathering (ENG) technologies. The use of portable cameras greatly simplified the process of news gathering, and hence made its work more efficient. Into the 1980s, computer technology was broadly applied in the production, broadcasting, and transmission of television shows.

The pioneering world news reform

The fundamental reform of television, however, was motivated by calls for the emancipation of the mind surrounding the Third Plenary Session of the 11th CPC Central Committee and Reform and Opening Up, and it began with the reform of world news reporting. At the start of 1979, CCTV concluded in a review of its world news that the coverage was narrow, piecemeal, partial, tardy, limited in sources, and restricted by too many "forbidden zones." Expansion was thus announced: all major international political activities and conferences, scientific research events, as well as major news of all aspects of life from other countries should be covered with objectivity and discretion.

The then Peking Television's *World News* (*Guoji xinwen* 國際新聞) premiered back in 1979, but it was largely a platform for disseminating Soviet newsreels and documentary movies. In the 1960s, television in China relied mainly on Visnews for news sources. In September 1979, CCTV finally signed an agreement with another news agency, UPITN, for exchanging news videos. At the same time, it was given the privilege of receiving Xinhua releases, alongside the Central People's Broadcasting Station, ahead of the newspapers. The releases were adopted in an additional news bulletin segment, which offered around eight headlines in a total of 1,000 words over five minutes, together with related news photos and background information, in *Xinwen Lianbo*.

Until April 1980, news exchange with Visnews and UPITN had been performed by airmail, which meant a two-week lag by the time the tapes arrived at the studio. With the development of satellite technology, news could reach Beijing from London and New York the next day after its release. While a technological breakthrough, the repercussions of this innovation soon proved to be far-reaching. In the same year, *World News* was made a part of *Xinwen Lianbo* and promoted as a big highlight of the show. More importantly, the advancement of television in world news reporting elevated the status of television as a news medium, inspiring the entire news industry.

The domestic news reform

While world news impressed the audience with extensive coverage of events on the other side of the world, domestic news on television was still comparatively dull and overdue. Such flaws were most expressed in *Xinwen Lianbo*, which had the support of most television channels in the country.

Xinwen Lianbo was predated by a newscast called *Television News* (*Dianshi xinwen* 電視新聞), which debuted in 1960 and became a simulcast in mid-1976. The 10-to-15-mintue show was all on domestic news, and the decision of simultaneous broadcasting failed to engender much change in its content. This was partly due to struggles with slow technological modernization. Microwave transmission of news had yet to be developed, and the simulcast network was defective. A year had to pass before Shanghai, Guangzhou, Hebei, Nanjing, Wuhan, Hunan, Henan, and Chengdu were able to return local news shows to Beijing via microwaves. News exchange between CCTV and some local television stations through microwave links was only formalized in 1980, in fulfillment of the 10th National Broadcasting Work Conference's verdict that local television stations be the collective journalists of CCTV.

The name *Xinwen Lianbo* (news simulcast), short for *Nationwide Television Stations News Simulcast* (*Quanguo dianshi xinwen tai lianbo* 全國電視新聞台聯播), was formally adopted in January 1978. In April 1981, the Central Broadcasting Bureau held a nationwide industry seminar in Qingdao regarding the running of this particular newscast: the show was to provide comprehensive and timely coverage of major domestic and international events.

The Qingdao seminar had two immediate effects. First, the construction of microwave transmission channels was sped up. Second, the program flow of *Xinwen Lianbo* was adjusted. Originally presented in three separate segments, domestic newsreels, world news reports, and satellite world news videos plus domestic news reports from the Central People's Broadcasting Station were reprogrammed according to the content of each particular piece. The reporting of each news item was shortened to make room for more events. There were also changes in the show's "cosmetics," such as the logo, backdrop, format of reporting headline news, and weather forecast graphics. Moreover, background music was deleted. As such, it broke away from the rigid newsreel format to become an integrated newscast.

In 1982, the movement of the most important news stories to 7 p.m. from 8 p.m. in *Xinwen Lianbo* showed that news could be released earlier in the medium of television than elsewhere. The reorganization of the Central Broadcasting Bureau into the Ministry of Radio and Television in the same year signaled a growth in the status of television broadcasting.

Follow-up reforms

Further reforms followed the first breakthroughs from the late 1970s to the beginning of the 1980s. In world news reporting, China entered into the news exchange scheme of the Asia-Pacific Broadcasting Union in April 1984. Moreover, CCTV received and recorded newscasts by the Taiwanese Chinese Television System through Xiamen Television Station in June 1984, and stationed correspondents in Hong Kong for the coverage of Hong Kong and Macau news in 1986. After that, it tried to expand its news sources by receiving news videos from the European Broadcasting Union, CNN, and the International Radio and Television Organization.

Within China, the frequency of news transmission increased from a few times per month to every day in 1986. Further adjustments were seen in the programming of CCTV. In 1984, it increased the broadcasting times of variety shows during daytime hours and launched *Noon News* (*Wujian xinwen* 午間新聞). This was followed by the introduction of *Evening News* (*Wanjian xinwen* 晚間新聞) in 1985, *English News* (*Yingyu xinwen* 英語新聞) in 1986, *Integrated Economic News* (*Zonghe jingji xinxi* 綜合經濟信息, later renamed *Half-Hour Economics* (*Jingji ban xiaoshi* 經濟半小時)) in 1987, and *Sports News* (*Tiyu xinwen* 體育新聞) in 1989. CCTV's second nationwide integrated program, *Integrated Economic News* was transmitted through the newly completed domestic communications satellite network.

Local television stations and local television news programs

The 11th National Radio and Television Work Conference convened in Beijing in the spring of 1983 designated television as the jumping-off point of the reform of radio and television propaganda. Apart from putting forward concrete proposals like setting up a news center and grooming multitalented journalists, it endorsed a momentous "four-level" television policy. By sanctioning the decentralized operation of television according to the administrative levels, the policy brought diversity into the previously uniform, top-down television structure. Moreover, policy opportunities coincided with the expansion of the commodity economy, a material source of vigor and vitality to the new local television businesses.

Once the green light was lit, local television stations sprang up like flowers in spring. Between 1983 and 1989, the total number of television broadcasters in China surged from 52 to 469, in which 1 was national, 31 were provincial, 231 were prefectural, and 206 were county-level. However, the proliferation could hardly be governed by quality control. Many television broadcasters, especially those at the county level, were plagued by financial strains and technological backwardness, and could only resort to banal video programs from overseas sources. Worse still, a lot of these programs were pirated or shown excessively, leading to copyright arguments or adverse competition for viewers and advertisements. Furthermore, in areas covered by only one or a few channels, there was sharp competition between television broadcasters of various levels. The comprehensive *Xinwen Lianbo* and propaganda programs by national and provincial television stations lost out to local newscasts that were dominated by stories on conferences spotlighting local officials and cadres, as well as entertainment shows.

At the same time, resourceful enterprises and corporations would not have missed the golden business opportunities opened up by the popular mass medium. They seized the new potential of cable television with the development of the second- and third-generation community antennas, giving birth to more than 500 cable television operators by the end of 1989.

Thus, a diverse and comprehensive television network had come into shape. To name two influential regional television companies, Guangdong Television became the first "southern window" bringing in news from abroad, and Shanghai Television had numerous innovative explorations. To increase their stakes in the competitive news market, the broadcasters were zealous in experimenting with the development of news shows. Soon, the formation of large economic zones inspired collaborative efforts among provincial and prefectural television operators. Regional banks of news stories were formed, breaking the top-down apparatus of television news transmission. The national news center no longer had a monopoly.

World news

Guangdong Television began its news reform in January 1981, launching a five-minute daily program called *Hong Kong and Macau Update* (*Gang'ao dongtai* 港澳動態). About a month later, it introduced *Across the World* (*Guoji zongheng* 國際縱橫), setting the precedent for local television stations reporting on international current affairs. Later, Shanghai Television's *Look at the World* (*Guoji wang* 國際望) premiering in 1983 proved even more influential. From then on, a raft of international newsmagazines emerged all over the country. Even CCTV developed *Today's World* (*Jinri shijie* 今日世界) in 1984.

Business news

Shanghai Television set the trend of service-oriented business news shows by putting up the first of its kind in late 1981, titled *Market Snaps* (*Shichang lüeying* 市場掠影). Tailored for the commodity economy and market stimulation, the program was warmly received by industrial producers, suppliers, sales agents, and ordinary consumers alike. In 1982, Guangdong Television followed with a similar show named *Market Rambling* (*Shichang manbu* 市場漫步), which featured a large amount of live business news reports.

Social news

In 1983, the Guangdong broadcaster rolled out two social news shows in a row: *Flowers of Civilization* (*Wenming zhi hua* 文明之花) and *Down in Records* (*Li ci cun zhao* 立此存照). The former commended exemplary personalities, deeds, and thoughts, while the latter criticized the unhygienic, misbehaved, and unethical. In 1984, the Shanghai broadcaster's *From the Audience* (*Guanzhong zhong lai* 觀眾中來), a short interactive program that investigated complaints from the audience, started the trend of news programs dedicated to answering questions, addressing dissatisfactions, and representing public voices.

News bulletins

In January 1982, Shanghai Television took the lead in presenting a second news bulletin, which took place in the evening, and Guangdong Television added a noon newscast in the following July. In 1983, Guangdong Television made the first attempt of live news broadcasts in China ever since the Cultural Revolution when it launched a new channel, making news broadcasting all live while retaining recorded voiceovers for news videos. After setting up an all-in-one news center for news gathering, recording, and editing in 1984, Shanghai Television also switched to live news broadcasts. Both broadcasters had up-to-standard news gathering equipment, communications technologies, and news vehicles that guaranteed smooth news reporting in times of accidents.

English news

Shanghai Television launched its first English news show in October 1986, two months ahead of CCTV.

Newsmagazines

The first major magazine-style news program by Shanghai Television, *News Perceptions* (*Xinwen toushi* 新聞透視), came after it pushed through the independent operation of its mutually competitive Channels One and Two in June 1986. Likewise, Guangdong Television launched the integrated news program *Morning* (*Zaochen* 早晨), which featured extensive news coverage and interviews.

The coverage of major political conferences and events

CCTV's groundbreaking news special *Documentary of the Reporting of the Sixth NPCSC* (*Liu jie quanguo renda changwei hui di shiqi ci huiyi caifang jishi* 六屆全國人大常委會第十七次會議採訪紀實) in September 1986 aroused great enthusiasm among the public. The positive response was due not only to its exploration of an issue of public concern — the introduction of the *Enterprise Bankruptcy Law*, but also its adoption of the documentary style. Such a transparent broadcast of the lively debates of NPCSC members was never-before-seen in China's television history. The program even featured the first-ever on-the-spot interview of NPCSC leaders, including Chairman Peng Zhen.

Since its first attempt generated letters of praise, CCTV lost no time in airing news updates of the Fifth Plenary Session of the Sixth NPC and CPPCC during March and April 1987, with the addition of videos of press conferences and state leaders' meetings with journalists, NPC delegates, and CPPCC members.

The CPC made a landmark gesture of political transparency by giving up the long-held confidentiality of its National Congress in October 1987. During the convention of this 13th Congress, 11 press conferences were staged, each of which was recorded and broadcast by CCTV. Henceforth, Party cadres and government officials had an increasing presence on television talk shows, and serial features on major political events, sometimes broadcast live with subtitles providing quick updates, became customary.

Overall improvements in news dissemination

Television dominated the National Outstanding Journalism Awards of 1986, winning two out of the three Top Grade Awards. The winning news stories were Sichuan Television's "Documentary of Adventures along Yangtze" and Hebei Television's "The Pursuit of a Blind Girl." The ascending role of television in news dissemination after Reform and Opening Up was reflected in the following aspects:

The increase in the amount of information

When simultaneous news broadcasting was first attempted in 1976, less than 10 news items were broadcast every day, each lasting for four to five minutes. In terms of content, monotonous reports on agricultural and industrial production and development were the rule. In the 1980s, each news item was reduced to around a minute in favor of wider news coverage. The number of news shows was also on the growth. Economic news was presented in more vivid styles, with greater connections to people's lives. Cultural, sports, technology, and entertainment news gained increasing attention, the proportion of social news substantially expanded, and serious criminal cases, accidents, and disasters were given significant coverage. Many local television channels featured social news every day, praising civilized behavior while criticizing dishonorable conduct. Lastly, the relaxation of world news broadcasting allowed Chinese citizens to stay informed about the world.

Improvement in timeliness

By the mid-1980s, the immediate reporting of accidental news was a common pursuit of television journalists, and it was enabled by the expansion of the news reporting teams and improvements in communications technology.

The diversity of program formats

Since Guangdong Television won two National Outstanding News Top Grade Awards in 1984 and 1985 with the serial features "Guangzhou Citizens Scrambled to Offer Blood to Injured Workers" and "20,000 Guangzhou Children Struggling for Primary School Places," serial reporting came into fashion. Also common were news series on a specific propaganda topic, such as CCTV's *In a Fingersnap* in celebration of the 40th founding anniversary of the People's Republic of China in 1989. In-depth critical news shows like *Observation and Reflection* (*Guancha yu sikao* 觀察與思考), also by CCTV, experimented with detailed explanations, investigations, and commentaries on current affairs. Moreover, the period witnessed the mature and flexible use of subtitles and images, which furthered the appeal of television shows.

The development of critical journalism

The first instance of critical news reporting on television was found in CCTV's "Observations from a Parking Lot in Wangfujing." Having experienced peaks and troughs of development, major critical news pieces won the recognition of the Outstanding Journalism Awards every year. Shanxi Television, for example, was acclaimed for its dedication in uncovering major policy flaws, such as the loss of credit control, black-hole projects, and loopholes in the family planning policy. Simplistic criticism had been replaced with multifaceted analysis which aimed to convince readers by reasoning.

Limitations in television news programs

In 1988, television in China celebrated its 30th birthday. However, after 30 years of development, some news programs had yet to break out of the frame of uniformity. There had to be more diverse perspectives of news, a better response to the multiple demands on information, more distinctive local characteristics in program development, and a greater number of quality opinion and in-depth news programs. Moreover, newsmagazines were underdeveloped. The worst was that in some news shows, the line between news and advertisements was blurred.

The development of other television programs

An integrative medium of cultural dissemination, television impacts on society and people's lives in numerous aspects through all kinds of programs. The days following 1979 saw the transitioning of television dramas from single shows into serials and sketch comedies, which topped the chart of popularity. Variety shows abounded in various forms, with that of the annual Spring Festival gala recording impressive ratings. Interactive and participatory programs such as competition shows caught on. Television documentaries were enlivened by artistic innovations, yielding exemplary pieces. General educational programs played a great part in raising the cultural level of society, inspiring talents that contributed to the development of the nation, and creating an atmosphere for learning. Some shows were tailored for, and managed to entice the hearts of specific demographic groups. Lastly, television in China bore the mission of facilitating the nation's cultural interaction and communication with the outside world.

Beyond television news and shows

As a side note, the popularization of video recording equipment meant that it was no longer exclusively owned by television operators. It was readily adopted by enterprises and organizations for publicity, documentation, education, and communication. It also gave rise to a bank of amateur news videos, which recorded many unexpected newsworthy moments. The most prominent example was Chengdu Institute of Radio Engineering's unintended capture of the historic forced landing of China Airlines Flight 334 in Guangzhou Baiyun International Airport under the hijacking of pilot Wang Xijue in 1986, which occurred during the recording of educational videos of takeoffs and landings.[31]

Photojournalism

Photojournalism evolved along the nation's policy change and shift of focus towards Socialist modernization. Breakthroughs were achieved in theories, practice, and education.

The rise of photojournalism societies and research on photojournalism theories

After 1979, how photojournalism could adapt to the nation's new developments and serve its Reform and Opening Up was the chief question facing the industry. In 1980, Xinhua's news photography department held three meetings discussing the characteristics and routines of photojournalism, the relationship between photojournalism and politics, as well as the connections and differences between Socialist and capitalist photojournalism. Freshness, truthfulness, and vividness were first identified as the "three pursuits" of photojournalists. Later, sensible characterization and accurate communication were added to the list. As such, the "five pursuits" became the prevailing gauge of photojournalism in China on top of the Four Cardinal Principles.

To enhance research on photojournalism theories, the Capital Journalism Studies Society set up a Photojournalism Group at the beginning of 1981, initiating a series of academic and professional activities for news units and photojournalists based in the capital. Specifically, its contributions to the reform of photojournalism in Beijing included representing the industry in participating in the national Outstanding Photojournalism Awards competition, organizing the 1981 Capital News Photo Exhibition, and holding meetings and seminars for the introduction of industry news, exchange of research findings, and promotion of pioneering experiences.

In 1983, the Photojournalism Group of the Capital Journalism Studies Society answered the requests of provincial news units for expanding the scope of its photography exhibition. The success of this National News Photo Exhibition, which showcased the outstanding shots of 1982, was extended into an annual exhibition tour starting from the following year. It also stimulated the mushrooming of similar local exhibitions, providing opportunities for the exchange of ideas while enriching the cultural life of the general public.

Between 1982 and early 1983, Tianjin, Anhui, Heibei, Shanxi, and Henan each set up their own photojournalism society or research group. In October 1983, the first national organization dedicated to photojournalism, the Photojournalist Society of China, finally appeared. In 1987, the society had 28 corporate members and close to 1,000 individual members. Apart from holding national news photo exhibitions, organizing and recommending Chinese news photos to enter the World Press Photo contest in the Netherlands, and publishing news photo albums, it also convened the National Photojournalism Theory Conference in Tianjin, Chuzhou (Anhui), and Hu County (Shaanxi) in 1983, 1985, and 1988, respectively. The conferences yielded three impressive essay collections, each of which comprised over 100 papers of fresh perspectives, including some on marginal topics. The contribution of young scholars to theory research generated high hopes for the future. A lot of essays were open to lessons from other countries, linking theories to actual practice. Even chief editors and presidents of some newspapers and news agencies submitted their papers. Indeed, this was the most prosperous period for the publication of monographs on photojournalism since the establishment of the People's Republic of China.

The photojournalism of China Daily and its impact

The founding of the English-language *China Daily* in 1981 brought a revolution to China's photojournalism. Its front page design was centered on the headline news photo. On the other pages, the standard photo size was as large as eight inches, the smallest being no less than six inches and the largest going up to a third of a page. Gone were dry and monotonous visual illustrations of policies and standardized photos of human beings and machines. The everyday life of commoners, and their psychology literally came under the lens. This urged representatives of news units in Beijing to meet in mid-1982 to discuss reform approaches for photojournalism modeled on *China Daily*. In July, the *People's Daily* started enlarging its photos and adjusting its layouts accordingly. Newspapers from all over the country soon followed.

The reform was by no means confined to changes in layouts. A remarkable step was the recognition of critical news photos as a means of combatting social evils and bureaucratism. The taboo of negative photos was gradually broken, as undesirable scenes were captured to arouse the attention of the authorities alongside propagandist images. In terms of composition by subject matter, the proportion of photos on foreign affairs and government conferences was reduced in favor of those reflecting people's lives and wishes. There was also an increase in the quantity of news photos that provided business information. In general, newsworthiness was improved as a result of timeliness. Public photography competitions run by newspapers brought in new sources of news photos, and provided platforms for the emergence of many outstanding works.

Debate on the Expedition photo collection

Expedition (*Chuzheng* 出征) was a collection of seven photos by Pan Ke and Hou Dengke that portrayed the saddening farewell between a Chinese soldier departing for the Lao Shan battlefront and his fiancée at a train station during the Sino-Vietnamese Border Conflicts in 1984. Captured from a fresh angle that highlighted human emotions, it invited vehement debate upon its appearance at the 1986 National News Photo Exhibition in Shanghai.

The conservative school dismissed the photos for their woeful mood, which failed to depict the traditional "revolutionary heroism and optimism" of the People's Liberation Army. It believed that the sentimental photos had watered down the positive image of the defensive war and misrepresented the warrior's identity as well as the mental state of most warriors. *Expedition* was also a propaganda disaster, as it would promote the dread of war and cause doubt about the voluntariness of the soldiers. Even the photography skills displayed were criticized as mediocre and unoriginal.[32]

More liberal opinions lauded the photo collection as an embodiment of "the type of the ambitious and visionary youth of the 80s." Time had shown that news photos could no longer be judged by the same criteria. As in art and literature, the orthodox portrayal of typical characters against a typical backdrop was unrealistic. Such opinions went as far as to argue for the intrinsic value of photojournalism as more than a political tool, and to criticize the restrictive taboos imposed by the principles of "Socialist photojournalism" until the emergence of more general subjects (as opposed to celebratory images) and some dark areas after the Third Plenary Session of the 11th CPC Central Committee. The change was a manifestation of the fading of traditional concepts.[33]

This was the first debate over the macro principles of photojournalism in three decades, although there had been discussion on the question of truthfulness on a case-by-case basis. Such a radical challenge to the traditional theoretical framework was previously unheard of despite the gradual changes brought by the Third Plenary Session of the 11th CPC Central Committee. Before any conclusion could be drawn, however, the debate was to continue for a while at the watershed between the old and the new, awaiting verification by experience.

The resumption and development of photography education

Suspended for a decade, photography training for working and potential photojournalists resumed towards the end of the 1970s. The news photography department of Xinhua organized two training courses over a month and a half in 1979 and 1982, respectively, for editors and reporters that had never received systematic training. Similarly, in 1982, the *Workers' Daily* held a two-month training workshop for about 60 photo correspondents with the aid of the Beijing Journalism Studies Society.

Observing that short-term training courses were not a sufficient antidote to the troubling quality of photojournalists in the long run, resourceful tertiary institutions launched specialized photography programs for them. Starting from 1983, colleges like the Renmin University of China, its first branch campus, and Jiangxi Normal University launched two-year photography programs for young working photographers one after another. Accepting the commission of Xinhua's photography department, Renmin University admitted 31 high school graduates into its undergraduate journalism program, which featured an expanded curriculum on photojournalism, through the National Higher Education Entrance Examination in 1985. The first direct collaboration between a news unit and a higher learning institution in talent grooming was realized.

By the late-1980s, around 40 public tertiary institutions had set up a journalism department or major that offered photography courses. In 1986, the School of Journalism of Renmin University added a four-year photojournalism major — the country's first higher-education program of its kind — upon approval by the State Education Commission. In 1985, the same university started running research master's degrees for the discipline. Theses on photojournalism made their first appearances in academic journals in 1983, after the first attempts by journalism graduates of Renmin University and Fudan University in 1981.

Soon, community societies, photography organizations, and private schools joined in the tide of setting up schools and providing classes of photography. As examples, the China Photographers Association and *PLA Pictorial* each founded their own correspondence school for photography in 1985, and the privately-run Haidian University added photojournalism to its undergraduate degrees in 1988.

Yet, the standards of tertiary-level photojournalism education had not always kept up with the speed of development. The insufficiency of qualified teachers, the lack of quality textbooks and teaching aids, and the backwardness of practice equipment and teaching methods were all problems that took time to be resolved.

Newsreels and documentaries

The emancipation of the mind embodied by the Third Plenary Session of the 11th CPC Central Committee eventually freed newsreels and documentary movies from the shackles of ultra-leftism. New subjects and methods of portraying them were explored to document the developments of the Four Modernizations.

Newsreels

As television broadcasts were timelier in coverage than newsreels, changes had to be made to their traditional forms of news reporting. In January 1978, the Central Newsreel and Documentary Film Studio replaced its *News Bulletin* (*Xinwen jianbao* 新聞簡報) collection, which had been running for 30 years, with the multicolor *New Look of the Motherland* (*Zuguo xin mao* 祖國新貌). Instead of filming current affairs and political news, the new series presented short and focused portrayals of everyday experiences through narratives and lyrical shots. A quick glance at the titles of its individual productions would provide an idea about the choice of subjects. Prominent examples included *Couple Running a Shop* (*Fuqi kaidian* 夫妻開店), *Big Hotel, Small Customers* (*Da fandian de xiao guke* 大飯店的小顧客), *A Foreign-Language Corner at a Park* (*Gongyuan li de waiyu jiao* 公園裡的外語角), *First Snow* (*Chuxue* 初雪), and *Worms Spitting Silk, Bees Brewing Honey* (*Can tu si feng niang mi* 蠶吐絲蜂釀蜜), where unique renditions of ordinary episodes created convincing movies with artistic appeal.

Documentary movies

Documentary movies reflected life in even more varied angles and through broader subjects. The increasing diversity in the choice of subjects and points of view manifested both the drastic changes in life and the emancipation of the minds of the producers. The spirits and values that characterized the age of Reform and Opening Up found particular expression in themes that had hardly been explored before.

The choice of subjects

A significant portion of the documentary movies produced after the Third Plenary Session of the 11th CPC Central Committee continued to be devoted to political propaganda, and a large number of them were about revolutionary personalities. Other than the full screening of the banned *Our Immortal Premier Zhou Enlai*, the likes of *Mao Zedong* (*Mao Zedong* 毛澤東), *Our Immortal Comrade Liu Shaoqi* (*Liu shaoqi tongzhi yongchuibuxiu* 劉少奇同志永垂不朽), and *NPC Chairman Zhu De Will Always Live in Our Hearts* (*Zhude weiyuan chang huo zai women xinzhong* 朱德委員長活在我們心中) were created to commemorate the glorious lives of the older generation of proletarian revolutionaries. The August First Film Studio's *Grand Contribution* (*Guanghui yeji* 光輝業績) documented the accomplishments of five marshals — namely, Zhu De, Peng Dehuai, He Long, Chen Yi, and Luo Ronghuan — all at once. The early contributions of some pre-Communist heroes were also celebrated in movies such as *Biography of Lu Xun* (*Lu xun chuan* 魯迅傳), *Gem of the Nation: Soong Ching-ling* (*Guozhi guibao — song qingling* 國之瑰寶——宋慶齡, and *Revolutionary Pioneer Sun Yat-sen* (*Geming xianxingzhe sun zhongshan* 革命先行者孫中山). Moreover, there were works directed against the wrongs of the Cultural Revolution, such as *Eyebrows Raised and Sword Unsheathed* (*Yangmei jian chu qiao* 揚眉劍出鞘), which reproduced the momentous mourning of Zhou in 1976, and *Golden Phoenixes upon a House of Bachelors* (*Jin fenghuang fei jin guanggun tang* 金鳳凰飛進光棍堂), which documented the rehabilitation of an ordinary family which had been labeled "landlords."

The People's Liberation Army was a frequent target of the Chinese documentary producers. During the 1979 Sino-Vietnamese Border Conflicts, the Central Newsreels and Documentary Film Studio and August First Film Studio sent a joint film shooting team to the battlefront, and the fruit of the expedition was *A Vigorous Fight-Back* (*Fenqi huanji* 奮起還擊). At the celebration of the 35th anniversary of the People's Republic of China, productions like *National Day Troop Review* (*Guoqing yuebing* 國慶閱兵) and *Before Troop Review* (*Shouyue zhiqian* 受閱之前) gave indirect portrayals of significant historical events. *Iron Great Wall* (*Gangtie changcheng* 鋼鐵長城), *Fly to the Pacific* (*Fei xiang taipingyang* 飛向太平洋), *Dragon over the Rainbow* (*Tenglong fei caihong* 騰龍飛彩虹), and *Deng Jiaxin: Father of Two Atomic Bombs* (*Liang dan yuanxun deng jiaxian* 兩彈元勳鄧稼先), among others, extolled the nation's military and scientific achievements.

Reform and Opening Up was itself a big theme of documentaries of the age. *Spring Starts Here* (*Chunfeng cong zheli chui qi* 春風從這裡吹起) publicized economic changes since the rural reform by capturing farmers carrying sacks of cash for trading in the market. Representations of industrial success included *To Begin with the Beibei Ball* (*Cong beibeiqiu shuo qi* 從貝貝球說起) about the transformation of a rubber factory manufacturing children's footballs, *Anshan and Anshan People* (*Anshan he anshan ren* 鞍山和鞍山人) and *Inspiring Careers* (*Cui ren fenfa de shiye* 催人奮發的事業) about the reform of steel plants, and *The Insight of Director Zhang* (*Zhang chang zhang de yangguang* 張廠長的眼光) about the rise of a local trench-coat brand. *The Window of Hope: Shenzhen* (*Xiwang de chuangkou — shenzhen* 希望的窗口——深圳) celebrated the prosperity of the featured Special Economic Zone. Some productions looked beyond the Chinese Mainland to express the party-state's sentiments about Hong Kong, Macau, and Taiwan. They included *100 Days in Hong Kong* (*Xianggang yibai tian* 香港一百天), *Suffering Macau* (*Aomen cangsang* 澳門滄桑), *Ah, Taiwan* (*A, taiwan* 啊，台灣), and *Feelings across the Taiwan Strait* (*Haixia qingsi* 海峽情思).

Apart from major political and economic themes, topics that were closer to people's lives also appeared on the screens. *Let the Years Not Flow away with Water* (*Mo rang nianhua fu shuiliu* 莫讓年華付水流) featured 10 ordinary youngsters of various professions, from factory workers to intellectuals, who persevered through hardship, whereas *Girls Under the Sea* (*Qian hai guniang* 潛海姑娘) zoomed in on the single, less common profession of marine culture. Featuring specific communities, *A Wonderful Gallery* (*Qimiao de hualang* 奇妙的畫廊) documented the development of science and art for children, while *Voices from the Heart* (*Xinsheng* 心聲) and *Strong Lives* (*Shenghuo de qiang zhe* 生活的強者) gave voice to the disabled and praised their resilience. In addition, a large number of sports movies had emerged, such as *Beautiful Wishes* (*Mei de xinyuan* 美的心願), *Stars over the Net* (*Wangshang qunxing* 網上群星), and *Zero to Breakthrough* (*Ling de tupo* 零的突破).

Stylistic breakthroughs

Documentary movies in this period were also invigorated by stylistic breakthroughs. Affecting details were depicted to highlight the significance of the subject. *Beautiful Melody* (*Mei de xuan lü* 美的旋律) on the Shanghai International Gymnastics Invitational Tournament departed from the conventional flat narrative style, revealing the beauty of sports through the physical movements and mental outlook of the athletes. *Narrative of an Old Beijinger* (*Lao Beijing de xueshuo* 老北京的敘說) offered an account of the Chinese capital that was at once solemnly historical and intensely contemporary, as it weaved together the past and present from the distinctive point of view of a local senior citizen.

The exposition of human emotions was the nexus of the new wave of news documentaries. Such temperaments that embodied the spirit of the age provided material for a kaleidoscope of documentary characters. In a humanistic vein, *The Spirit of the Cactus* (*Xianrenzhang jingshen* 仙人掌精神) looked into the endeavors of biologist Zhang Xiangtong, *A Drop in the Ocean* (*Canghaiyisu* 滄海一粟) presented the everyday labor of People's Liberation Army soldiers, *Sparkling Youth* (*Shanguang de qingchun* 閃光的青春) paid tribute to sanitation workers, *Etched into the Black Fertile Land* (*Ke zai hei wo de tudi shang* 刻在黑沃的土地上) recorded the contributions of those devoting their youthful years to the development of border areas, and *Let the Years Not Flow Away with Water* presented the struggles of youngsters pondering about their future.

Documentary production in the New Era was characterized by diverse styles and forms. *Bamboo* (*Zhu* 竹), which eulogized steadfast and noble characters symbolized by the plant of the title, impressed audiences with idyllic charm. *Superstar Weiwei* (*Chaoji mingxing weiwei* 超級明星偉偉) used editing and design to piece together the humorous movements and facial expressions of Weiwei the panda. *Blue Sky Lyric* (*Lantian shuqing* 藍天抒情) provided a bird's-eye view of China's magnificent landscape, which unfolded alongside the reading of a long poem. Landscape documentaries formed a genre of their own, with some examples being *Wonders of Huangshan* (*Huangshan guan qi* 黃山觀奇), *The Only Path Up Mount Hua* (*Zigu huashan yitiao lu* 自古華山一條路), and *Reverie of Jiuzhaigou* (*Jiuzhaigou menghuan qu* 九寨溝夢幻曲).

The popularity of serial reporting in television inspired a similar genre in cinema production: the documentary series. *Happy Travelling* (*Yukuai de lüxing* 愉快的旅行) introduced scenic spots and special customs within China, while the *Roam around the World* (*Manyou shijie* 漫遊世界) series travelled to places outside the country. On history, *Modern Spring and Autumn* (*Jindai chunqiu* 近代春秋) recounted the details of China's contemporary revolutions, and *Forbidden City, Beijing* (*Beijing zijincheng* 北京紫禁城) covered the valuable and eye-pleasing treasures of the Palace Museum. Also notable was the *China* (*Zhongguo* 中國) series which offered the largest-scale introduction of China to date.

International exchange

In 1980, the Central Newsreels and Documentary Film Studio crafted the slogan "Facing the whole country, facing the world" and started producing works that reached out to international audiences. At the same time, it also sent professionals overseas for filming and conducting movie research. Acclaimed externally-distributed movies included *China Vistas* (*Zhongguo fengmao* 中國風貌), *The Warm*

Spring of Jinling (*Jinling chunnuan* 金陵春暖), and the above-mentioned *China*.

News media administrative agencies

The Chinese government set up two agencies to enhance the administration of the journalism businesses that flourished after the Third Plenary Session of the 11th CPC Central Committee: the State Press and Publication Administration and the Ministry of Radio, Film, and Television.

The State Press and Publication Administration

Changes swept through China's newspaper industry in the 1980s. Many special-interest papers that were not Party organs had entered the industry structure. It became inappropriate and unfeasible to keep them all under the helm of local Party committees and their propaganda departments. The need for a specialized body capable of providing specific guidance and handling the planning, organization, and control of the overall industry was evident. Finally, after repeated proposals by the News Bureau of the CPC Propaganda Department, the State Council set out to establish the State Press and Publication Administration in January 1987.

Directly placed under the State Council, the Press and Publication Administration was mainly in charge of the administration of the nation's print media, i.e., newspapers and periodicals. In other words, radio broadcasters, television operators, and news agencies were not within its scope of control. It had four major functions: first, undertaking the overall planning of the industry, including approving new publications and regulating the industry structure; second, creating and implementing rules and regulations; third, investigating and handling illegal publication activities; and fourth: the macro-administration of the newspaper and publication businesses.

After its establishment, the State Press and Publication Administration made two streamlining adjustments to the nation's print media in 1987 and 1989. They were necessitated by the rampant proliferation in the prior decade. Statistically, between 1978 and 1988, the number of newspapers surged by 1,500, at a rate of two per five days, and that of periodicals by 4,000, meaning two new publications were added every three days.[34] However, the editorial strength of the press fell far behind the speed of development. Nor could the capacity for paper production meet the demand of the expanded business. The latter problem culminated in a paper supply shortage in 1988.

The two adjustments were executed based on the following priorities: The top priority went to major newspapers and periodicals with wide social benefits and influence. The second to be valued and supported were those that belonged to the economic category, including those bearing the role of domestic and international economic propaganda outlets. Third, service papers were to be given enough room for development as long as they were healthy and popular, as they were closely associated with the everyday lives of the people and depended mainly on the consumers' money rather than state support.

Apart from cutting down on the size of the industry, the Press and Publication Administration also completed the reregistration of reporting stations and replacement of press passes. By the end of 1990, 939 reporting stations had been reregistered, and 74,254 press passes that were valid throughout the country had been issued. In addition, the Administration had issued 6,355 special passes for contributing reporters.

As there had been no attempt at press legislation, the administration of newspapers and publications had only been governed by ad hoc instructions and commands issued by the Party. In view of the massive expansion of the print media, the government embarked on legislative preparations in 1984, when the NPC Education, Science, Culture and Public Health Committee and the Institute of Journalism Studies of the Chinese Academy of Social Sciences cofounded an organization for media law research. The establishment of the Press and Publication Administration was closely followed by the setup of a media law drafting group, which comprised, in addition to the Administration itself, representatives from the CPC Propaganda Department, Xinhua, the *People's Daily*, the Ministry of Radio, Film and Television, the All-China Journalists Association, the Institute of Journalism Studies of the Chinese Academy of Social Sciences, and the Department of Journalism of the Renmin University of China in 1988. By the end of the year, the Office of the Media Law Drafting Group had completed the first draft of the law. Before its enactment, the Press and Publication Administration promulgated the *Provisional Regulations on Newspaper Management* (*Baozhi guanli zhanxing guiding* 報紙管理暫行規定) in December 1990, which laid down concrete regulations on the principles of Socialist newspaper running, the procedures for the examination and approval of new publications, and the methods of managing publication activities. The regulation denoted the commencement of formal press administration on a legal basis.

Soon, most provincial administrative divisions began reviewing the performance of the local press according to the *Provisional Regulations*, promoting well-performing organizations, providing suggestions to substandard ones, and giving criticism and punishment where necessary. The reviews were sometimes undertaken under the joint control of the local press administrative body and the propaganda department of the local Party committee, and sometimes only by the administrative body. Many provinces set up a particular committee for this purpose, hiring extra reviewers for the job. Some of these committees even issued publications regarding their review work. Such reviews were greatly valued by the local leadership, both as a channel to grasp public opinion and as a means to improve the quality of the press.

The prevalence of illegal publishing after Reform and Opening Up urged the new Press and Publication Administration to crack down on three particular types of activities:

- Publishing without a publication right, forging or misappropriating the name of an approved publication unit, or publishing without naming the publication unit;
- Publishing reactionary, obscene, or other prohibited content; and
- Publishing beyond the approved business scope, selling the *kanhao* (authorized publication number), or partaking in other behavior that violated the regulations on publication.

In response to the industry's struggles against financial stringency in the face of escalating circulation fees and paper costs, which was aggravated by the reduction of state subsidies, the Press and Publication Administration formulated and promulgated the *Provisional Rules Concerning Newspaper Publishers, Periodical Publishers and Publishing Houses Launching Paid-For Services and Commercial Activities (Guanyu baoshe, qikan she, chuban she kaizhan youchang fuwu he jingying huodong de zhanxing banfa* 關於報社、期刊社、出版社 開展有償服務和經營活動的暫行辦法) together with the State Administration for Industry and Commerce in 1988, sanctioning the operation of a range of businesses under the approval of related departments. Moreover, the Press and Publication Administration enforced a national newspaper price increase in January 1989, which lifted many newspapers from loss to profit.

The Ministry of Radio, Film, and Television

The overwhelming expansion of the radio and television sector in China has been detailed in previous sections. By the end of 1990, the two forms of media reached 74.7% and 79.4% of the population, respectively. Their pace of development, and their resulting significance in Socialist modernization, pointed to the need for better leadership and administration. As early as May 1982, the Fifth NPC passed the *Decision on the Implementation of the Reform of the Organizational Structure of the Ministries and Commissions of the State Council* (*Guanyu guowuyuan buwei jigou gaige shishi fang'an de jueyi* 關於國務院部委機構改革實施方案的決議), which endorsed the abolition of the Central Broadcasting Bureau, the establishment of the Ministry of Radio and Television (restructured as the Ministry of Radio, Film, and Television in 1986), and the appointment of Minister Wu Lengxi.

The Ministry was set up to provide centralized leadership over the nation's radio and television industries. Its scope of leadership and administration included: first, the domestic and international propaganda of the Central People's Broadcasting Station, China Radio International, CCTV, and all other radio and television operators; second, the China Record Corporation and China Radio and Television Publishing House's publication and circulation of books, magazines, audio products, and audio-visual products; and third, the China Broadcasting Performing-Arts Troupe and China Teleplay Production Center's program production. In addition, the Ministry had subdivisions overseeing foreign affairs related to radio and television broadcasting, as well as the publication and circulation of audio and audio-visual products in general.

The principle of "walking on one's own legs" was brought up a few times after Reform and Opening Up, first in the 10th National Broadcasting Work Conference of October 1980. The second time took place in 1982, after the establishment of the Ministry of Radio and Television, together with the new idea of "opening the door for radio and television" through gathering various forces in society. The third occasion was the 11th National Radio and Television Work Conference, where one more slogan — "Leverage the unique strengths of oneself, collect the essence of others" — was announced to reiterate the principle. Extra "forces" and "essence" from other sectors were necessary because the capacity of the broadcasters alone was insufficient to accommodate the diverse functions, varying types of programs, and long broadcasting hours they were expected to bear. The conference decided on the principles and policies of reforming and developing the radio and television media, with specific targets to be attained by 2000. The main goals were the comprehensive reform of news propaganda and the mixed coverage of national and local broadcasting services over all four levels of administrative divisions. The effects of reform and development, from the improvement of program types to the broadening of coverage, need not be repeated. By the end of 1990, the number of radio and television workers across the nation had grown to 300,000.

Journalism organizations

After the Third Plenary Session of the 11th CPC Central Committee, the reactivation of dormant journalism organizations was followed by the creation of new ones. Journalists' associations and journalism societies spanned the entire country, becoming a hallmark of the 1980s.

Journalists' associations

Soon after the All-China Journalists Association resumed its work in 1980, its provincial-level counterparts also went back to activity. In addition, there were organizations set up for specific groups of journalists, such as the Chinese Sports Journalists' Association (*Zhongguo tiyu jizhe xiehui*), Chinese Evening Paper Workers' Association (*Zhongguo wanbao gongzuo zhe xiehui*), Chinese Young Newspaper Workers' Association (*Zhongguo qingnian baokan gongzuo zhe xiehui*), and Capital Women Journalists' Association (*Shoudu nü xinwen gongzuo zhe xiehui*). Called to pay attention to both internal training and external liaisons, national and local journalists' associations launched various initiatives to enhance the overall performance of the industry.

Internal training

To begin with, business seminars, theory conferences, and experience exchange meetings were frequent platforms for interactions among journalists and news organizations. They also served as engines of journalism reform.

Another major initiative was the provision of direct training to journalists. The All-China Journalists Association set the example of introducing a journalism training course in 1982, which was expanded into a higher institute of journalism in the following year. In 1984, the institute was accredited by the Ministry of Education, and renamed the College of Journalism of the All-China Journalists Association. From 1982 to 1989, it produced 409 graduates for the industry. At the same time, the Association also ran short-term courses for working journalists who never had the chance to be educated at an institute of higher learning.

Journalists' associations also recognized the acknowledgement of outstanding performance as an incentive for improvement. In 1981, the All-China Journalists Association worked with its fellow co-organizers of the 1980 National Outstanding Journalism Awards, the Beijing Journalism Studies Society (the former Capital Journalism Studies Society) and the Editorial Department of *The Press*, to expand the scope of the competition. In addition to picking out particular news pieces, the Association also recognized individual journalists who had made special contributions to society through holding the National Outstanding Journalists' Commendation Conferences. Moreover, as it was a journalist who gave his life for defending his companion while wrestling with four gangsters that inspired the honoring of Outstanding Journalists, the All-China Journalists Association showed particular commitment to the cause of defending journalists' rights. Such efforts included organizing seminars that drew attention to cases where journalists were beaten at work and demanding that government departments punish the criminals.[35]

Finally, the adoption of the *Professional Ethical Standards for Chinese News Workers* (*Zhongguo xinwen gongzuo zhe zhiye daode zhunze* 中國新聞工作者職業道德準則) in the fourth board of directors' meeting of the All-China Journalists Association in January 1991 gave journalists a formal professional code of ethics. The guidelines included serving the people wholeheartedly; abiding by the law and acting with discipline; defending the truthfulness of news with fairness and objectivity; upholding integrity; maintaining the spirit of solidarity and collaboration; and fostering international cooperation.

External liaisons

Between China and the outside world, journalists' associations served as a window of understanding as well as a bridge of friendship. The All-China Journalists Association, in particular, played an important role in establishing friendship with journalists in Taiwan, Hong Kong, and Macau. When the first batch of Taiwanese journalists set foot on the Mainland in 1987, the Association was entrusted with the responsibility of assisting with their reporting duties. Later on, it continued to play host to journalists from Taiwan, Hong Kong, and Macau coming to cover the NPC, CPPCC, and CPC Central Committee, organizing representatives of the conferences, officials of the State Council, and other state leaders to brief these journalists about issues discussed in the meetings as well as the general conditions of China's economic reform and people's lives. In fact, the All-China Journalists Association also arranged press conferences that introduced China's economic policies and changes after Reform and Opening Up for foreign correspondents in Beijing all year round. The speakers of these press conferences included spokespersons of government departments and mass organizations.

Apart from receiving incoming journalists, the All-China Journalists Association and other local journalists' associations sent reporters to other countries to build friendships with journalism organizations. The Association had a particularly high regard for connections with journalists of the Third World, which motivated it to accept UNESCO's invitation to organize a seminar regarding journalism in developing countries in 1987.

Journalism societies

The vehement debate over lessons learned from the development of journalism in the first three decades of the People's Republic of China as well as the theory and practice of proletarian journalism formed the backdrop of the Capital Journalism Academic Symposium of October 1979, which gave birth to the Beijing Journalism Studies Society (*Beijing xinwen xuehui*) in February 1980. The Society was renamed the Capital Journalism Studies Society (*Shoudu xinwen xuehui*) in 1984 in order to avoid confusion with the newly founded Beijing Municipal Journalism Studies Society (*Beijing shi xinwen xuehui*), as journalism societies of various administrative and professional divisions came into being. Major specialized nationwide journalism societies included the China Radio and Television Society (*Zhongguo guanbo dianshi xuehui*), Photojournalist Society of China (*Zhongguo xinwen sheying xuehui*), China Journalism Education Society (*Zhongguo xinwen jiaoyu xuehui*), China Public Health News Society (*Zhongguo weisheng xinwen xuehui*), China Society for the Study of Science and Technology Press (*Zhongguo keji bao yanjiu hui*), China Sports News Society (*Zhongguo tiyu xinwen xuehui*), China Society for the Study of Worker Newspapers and Magazines (*Zhongguo gongren baokan yanjiu hui*), and Smedley-Strong-Snow Society of China (*Zhongguo san s yanjiu hui*, which studied the works of American reporters and writers Agnes Smedley, Anna Louise Strong, and Edgar Snow). At the end of 1984, an umbrella organization called the *Federation of Chinese Journalism Societies* (*Zhongguo xinwen xuehui lianhe hui*) was founded to coordinate journalism research of these societies at a national level. The first real national journalism academic body, the Chinese Association for History of Journalism and Mass Communication (*Zhongguo xinwen shi xuehui*), was formally established in 1992.

Academic conferences

Facilitating the exchange of research findings was a common mission of all journalism societies. To take the Beijing Journalism Studies Society as an example, it organized close to 100 academic conferences and seminars within the first four years after its foundation. Among them were large-scale symposiums in commemoration of the 100th anniversary of the death of Marx and the 90th birthday of Mao, as well as conferences dedicated to the journalism ideology of Liu Shaoqi and the coverage of economic news. Conferences on a smaller scale were by no means lesser in significance. Instead, they demonstrated a greater diversity, accommodating not only topics regarding the coverage of all types of news, but also broader issues such as journalism education, media legislation, readers' surveys, and the operations of the newspaper businesses. To increase the depth of studies, the Beijing Journalism Studies Society identified several areas where both ends of a research spectrum were to be taken into consideration: theory and practice, capitalist and proletarian journalism, professional and amateur research, as well as major and minor subjects. Academic research should mainly be driven by individual efforts with the support of organized activities.

In addition to organizing domestic events, journalism societies embraced opportunities of academic exchange with visiting scholars from other countries, inviting them to speak at seminars and conferences. The Beijing Journalism Studies Society, for example, participated twice in the Symposium on Chinese and Australian Journalism held in Beijing in 1981.

Journalism awards

The annual Outstanding Journalism Awards competition quickly turned into a major industry event in the 1980s. The first competition was the fruit of the concerted efforts of the Beijing Journalism Studies Society and *The Press*. Later, the team of co-organizers was joined by the slightly younger Federation of Chinese Journalism Societies. Other journalism societies held similar contests at local levels and for specific divisions of journalism. Every year, the winning news pieces were compiled into print publications for public appreciation.

Audience and industry surveys

Conducted with scientific methodology and technology, the plentiful audience surveys and surveys about the news industry in the 1980s were welcomed for their credibility. Some audience surveys targeted the audience of a particular news medium or news organization, while others focused on a specific topic. The first to make use of modern statistical methods was a sampling survey of Beijing's news audience by the Beijing Journalism Studies Society in 1982, which provided the basis for the first-ever integrated study of a region's audience. In 1985, the Society made another breakthrough by undertaking the first quantitative analysis of China's newspapers.

Journalism publications

Many journalism societies had their own publications. For example, the Beijing Journalism Studies Society published the *Newsletter of the Beijing Journalism Studies Society* (*Xinwen xuehui tongxun* 新聞學會通訊) upon its foundation, and the Federation of Chinese Journalism Societies the *News Journal* (*Xinwen xuekan* 新聞學刊).

Journalism education

During the Cultural Revolution, student recruitment of all journalism programs was put to a halt, causing tremendous disruption to journalism education. As a result, the boom of the news industry after the smashing of the Gang of Four only made manpower shortages more acute. Fortunately, the vacuum was quickly filled following the Third Plenary Session of the 11th CPC Central Committee.

The resumption and introduction of tertiary journalism education

The restoration of journalism education was set off by the resumption of the National Higher Education Entrance Examination in 1977, with which Peking University, Fudan University, the Beijing Broadcasting Institute, and Guangxi University started recruiting journalism students again. In 1978, the Renmin University of China reopened its doors, as did its Department of Journalism, while Jinan University extended the availability of its newly resumed journalism major to students from Hong Kong and Macau. In the days that followed, all provincial universities that had run journalism programs, including Zhengzhou University, Jiangxi Normal University, Hangzhou University, and Tianjin Normal University, began recruiting students again. Some other tertiary institutions, such as the Institute of International Politics in Beijing, Hebei University, Sichuan University, Anhui University, and Shanxi University, added journalism to their major programs, often managed by a brand new journalism department. To catch up with the development of radio and television, many institutes introduced or reintroduced broadcast journalism majors on top of the existing technical programs. By the end of 1982, 16 higher education institutes had been offering journalism majors, admitting a total of 1,585 students, who were trained by 364 teachers.

At the same time, Deng Xiaoping's famous statement that "without grasping science and education, there can be no hope for the Four Modernizations" in September 1977 prompted the resumption of research postgraduate degrees within a month. In 1978, the Graduate School of the Chinese Academy of Social

Sciences recruited 85 journalism research students. Adding up the intake of Remin University (8) and Fudan University (4), a total of 97 journalism postgraduates were admitted in the year. With the introduction of the degree system in 1981, most of the 1978 class were conferred a Master's degree. In 1985, Renmin University and Fudan University went on to take on the first six doctoral research students for Journalism Studies, taking journalism education to the next level.

The National Seminar on Journalism Education and the expansion of tertiary journalism education

In May 1983, the CPC Propaganda Department and the state's Ministry of Education joined to convene the first National Seminar on Journalism Education, which investigated the planning and reform of journalism education. Before the seminar, the organizers had conducted surveys about the current state of journalism education and the industry's demand for new blood, as well as interviewed senior journalists and other leaders of the industry. The investigation found that while China had as many as 260,000 news workers, the pace of talent grooming fell significantly short of the demand. From the beginning of the People's Republic of China until then, only 5,200 journalism graduates had been produced, and the actual number assigned to news units was down to 3,000. However, according to the forecast put forward in the conference, the expanded newspapers, news agencies, radio stations, and television stations would need a replenishment of as many as 74,000 graduates by the end of the 20th century. Taking into account the 20% that were to serve the Propaganda Department and other government bodies, the ideal number of total graduates needed would be 90,000, which equaled an average of 5,000 per year. The intake of higher education institutions at the time, in comparison, was merely 1,802, undergraduates, research postgraduates, and students of certificate programs included.

In view of the severe shortage, the Department of Propaganda and Ministry of Education issued the *Opinions on the Strengthening of Journalism Education* (*Guanyu jiaqiang xinwen jiaoyu gongzuo de yijian* 關於加強新聞教育工作的意見) in the following August, which stressed both the fast expansion of journalism education and the improvement of education quality. The effect of the document was immediate: the goal that every large administrative division should have at least one institute of higher learning that offered journalism majors by 1985 was attained ahead of time. With the response of Jilin University, Lanzhou University, Xinjiang University, Ningxia University, Wuhan University, the Huazhong Institute of Technology, and Xiamen University, the number of tertiary journalism education providers had shot up from 14 to 21 by the end of the year. The size of the teaching staff had expanded to 518 persons, while the total number of students had increased to 2,814.

The predicted demand at the turn of the century was satisfied by a comprehensive range of programs. At the end of 1989, there were 51 providers of major programs in journalism among China's tertiary institutions. To do a quick breakdown of their professional divisions, five offered a major in world news, five in broadcast journalism, three in photojournalism, two in broadcast anchoring and announcing, two in advertising, and one in radio and television. Over 5,000 students were studying for their journalism degrees, under the guidance of 880 full-time teachers.

Correspondence schools and courses

Flourishing alongside professional journalism programs were after-hours correspondence courses. The first correspondence school devoted to journalism was a "periodical correspondence university" (*kanshou xuexiao* 刊授學校), one that delivered courses through mailed periodicals, founded by the *Anhui Daily* in 1984, and it managed to recruit 20,000 students in a short period. Its success was soon followed by other newspaper groups, universities, and a research institute, giving birth to 11 journalism correspondence schools (see Table 23.10). The total enrollment of their courses was estimated to be over 130,000. With basically no restriction in geographic, social, and professional backgrounds, they had a wide appeal among cadres of propaganda departments, correspondents, and non-professionals interested in journalism. Sometimes, occasional face-to-face tutorials were arranged to enhance support for students.

Table 23.10 Correspondence journalism education in the 1980s

Course provider 1	Course provider 2	Name of school, department, or program
Anhui Daily	—	Correspondence University of Journalism (*Xinwen kanshou daxue*)
China Farmers' News	Department of Journalism, Renmin University of China	Farmers' Journalism Correspondence School (*Nongmin xinwen hanshou xuexiao*)
China Youth Daily	Department of Languages, Renmin University of China	Major in Journalism, Beijing Renwen Correspondence University (*Zhongguo renwen hanshou daxue*)

(Cont'd)

Course provider 1	Course provider 2	Name of school, department, or program
Economic Daily	—	Major in Economic News, Department of Economic Talent Development (*Jingji rencai kaifa hanshou bu*)
Gansu Research Institute of Journalism	Department of Journalism, Lanzhou University	Gansu Correspondence College of Journalism (*Gansu xinwen kanshou xueyuan*)
Heilongjiang Daily	—	Department of Correspondence Studies in Journalism (*Xinwen hanshou bu*)
Jilin Daily	—	Journalism Correspondence Training Institute (*Xinwen kanshou jiangxi suo*)
Liaoning Daily	—	Journalism Correspondence Education Center (*xinwen hanshou zhongxin*)
Nanfang Daily	Department of Journalism, Jinan University	Correspondence Education Center for Journalism Studies (*Xinwen xue kanshou zhongxin*)
People's Daily	—	Department of Correspondence Studies, Journalism Intellectual Development Center (*Xinwen zhili kaifa zhongxin*)
Shaanxi Daily	—	Northwest Correspondence College of Journalism (*Xibei xinwen kanshou xueyuan*)
Workers' Daily	Department of Journalism, Renmin University of China	Institute of Journalism of China (*Zhonghua xinwen hanshou xueyuan*)

Training courses for working journalists

Many news units started organizing training courses for their employees after 1983, and a portion of them set up training bases. In July 1984, the News Bureau of the CPC Propaganda Department and the All-China Journalists Association cohosted a training and work experience exchange meeting for journalists across the nation. In October of the same year, the Propaganda Department's *Vision on the Building of the Journalism Team* (*Xinwen duiwu jianshe guihua shexiang* 新聞隊伍建設規劃設想) was published to provide a written guideline on the training of working journalists. The China Journalism Education Society, which aimed to facilitate research on journalism education, was also founded in 1984.

Journalism education reform

To cultivate journalists in support of Socialist Modernization, schools of journalism across the country all sped up their efforts to explore reform of journalism education after the start of the Reform and Opening Up era. Most of them found it necessary to enhance the political and professional education of students. Political ideologies were to be taught with added strength to ensure a guaranteed level of understanding of the Party's policies and principles. On the professional side, students should be guided to reflect on the realistic problems in actual practice and be given substantial practical training. Moreover, it was generally agreed that more electives should be included in the curricula, so that students could gain a wider exposure in various fields of journalism. In the midst of reform, second degrees in journalism gained increasing prominence, as specialized knowledge beyond the field of journalism was found helpful to a journalist's work.

Regarding the journalism educators, improvements in quantity and quality were encouraging. A rough survey at the end of 1989 showed that China had a team of around 40 professors, 240 associated professors, 300 lecturers, and 260 teaching assistants, many of them accomplished researchers in the theory, history, and business of journalism. There were also modifications of the teaching materials. At the time of this writing, over 40 teaching packages have been developed according to the guidance set out in the Seventh Five-Year Plan of the State Education Commission. The major curricula are gradually supported by corresponding teaching and reference materials.

As the journalism education sector began to expand to a state in which quality was sometimes compromised, the State Education Commission directed two mild streamlining efforts in 1989 and 1990. Alongside those, the Propaganda Department of the CPC held a work seminar for chief editors of all provincial-level newspapers in November 1989, where Jiang Zemin and Li Ruihuan spoke about ideological principles that determined the direction of future journalism education reform. Consequently, curricula on journalism theories were reformed to bring in more Marxist elements, and new courses on Marxist journalism theory were introduced. Besides, many journalism schools emphasized the practical aspect of education, and therefore linked up with news organizations to provide opportunities for hands-on experience in conducting social surveys.

The November 1989 seminar was followed by many other workshops in the 1990s, not only by the central CPC Propaganda Department, but also many provincial propaganda departments, the State Press and Publication Association, news units like Xinhua and *Workers' Daily*, and the College of Journalism of the

All-China Journalists Association. With specific groups of journalists in mind, these seminars and workshops were held for the cultivation of professional ethics, which was fused with ideological education.

Journalism research

After the Third Plenary Session of the 11th CPC Central Committee, journalism research prospered under the blessings of emerging journalism research institutions. Research activities provoked vivid academic discussions on a broad range of topics. A plentitude of scholarly works and periodicals on journalism were yielded out of the frequent exchange of ideas and diligent efforts of researchers.

The establishment of research institutions

In August 1978 was born China's first national journalism research institute, the Institute of Journalism Studies of the Chinese Academy of Social Sciences. This symbolized the formal inclusion of journalism research into the nation's scientific research endeavors, and inaugurated a series of similar institutions at the provincial administrative divisions. The practice was also picked up by many national news units, including Xinhua, *People's Daily*, *Guangming Daily*, *Workers' Daily*, the Central People's Broadcasting Station, China Radio International, and CCTV, as well as the major provincial-level news units. Tertiary institutions, surely, did not miss out on the new research trend. The Renmin University of China established an Institute of Public Opinions, Fudan University created a Center for Journalism Studies under its Department of Journalism, and the Beijing Broadcasting Institute founded a News Research Center, for instance. These research institutions dug deep into fundamental theories on journalism through organizing domestic and international academic activities as well as publishing books and periodicals.

The content of research

The "blooming of a hundred flowers" and "contention of a hundred schools of thought" in journalism research actually began to take shape after the Third Plenary Session of the 11th CPC Central Committee. The expanded fields of research revolved around the six main aspects of journalism theory, the history of journalism, the business of journalism, journalism reform and media legislation, foreign journalism and communication studies, and news audiences. In addition, there were interdisciplinary studies on topics such as journalism literature, journalism aesthetics, and psychology in journalism.

Research on journalism theory

The first step of research on journalism theory was the correction of what had been upset and put into confusion by Lin Biao and the Gang of Four. In a symposium on journalism theory co-hosted by the Institute of Journalism Studies of the Chinese Academy of Social Sciences and the Beijing Journalism Studies Society in December 1980, the errors of ultra-leftism were clarified. In the decade that followed, a broad range of subjects regarding journalism theory were tackled in academic research and discussions. The long list included: the nature, mission, and functions of journalism; the "Party spirit" and "people spirit" of Party papers; the truthfulness of news; the role of news in providing guidance; news criticism and supervision by public opinion; journalism reform; media legislation; the relationship between news and propaganda; the renewal of the concept of journalism; the definition of news; the value of news; and Western communication studies.

In the aftermath of the Cultural Revolution, Party documents and speeches from Party leaders on journalism were highly valued. Jiang Zemin and Li Ruihuan's speeches in 1989 became the yardsticks for research in journalism theory, especially the study of Marxist canons. In March 1983, the first academic conference on the theory and practice of Marx's journalism ideology was held in remembrance of the 100th anniversary of his death. In a similar vein, the National Journalism Academic Conference in Memory of the 90th Birthday of Mao Zedong the following December sought a comprehensive understanding of Mao's journalism theory and discussed ways of putting it into practice, the fruit of which was recorded in *Research on Mao Zedong's Journalism Theory* (*Mao Zedong xinwen lilun yanjiu* 毛澤東新聞理論研究). Moreover, a series of works expounding the journalism ideologies of the late leaders were compiled to provide the cornerstones of research, including *Marx and Engel's Views on Journalism* (*Makesi en'gesi lun xinwen* 馬克思恩格斯論新聞), (*Marxist-Leninist Journalism Classics* 馬列主義新聞學經典論著), *A Study of Mao's Journalism Ideology* (*Mao zedong xinwen sixiang yanjiu* 毛澤東新聞思想研究), *Selected Works of News Activities of Mao Zedong* (*Mao zedong xinwen gongzuo wenxuan* 毛澤東新聞工作文選), and *Collection of Reports of the China Communist Party's News Activities* (*Zhongguo gongchandang xinwen gongzuo wenjian huibian* 中國共產黨新聞工作文件匯編).

Research on the history of journalism

To make up for the damage of historical sources done by the Cultural Revolution, researchers lost no time in recovering the general history, dynastic history, chronicle, and local history of China's journalism after Reform and Opening Up.

The study and writing of local journalism history paralleled that of local general history. Research on major long-living newspapers, such as *Xinhua Daily* (*Xinhua ribao* 新華日報), *Ta Kung Pao* (*Dagongbao* 大公報), *Shun Pao* (*Shenbao* 申報), and *Liberation Daily*, also gained momentum. Even the once neglected area of historical figures of the industry was extensively studied. Up to the 1991 edition, the "Chinese Journalism Figures" section of the *China Journalism Yearbook* had introduced 1,217 personalities and published a number of renowned journalists' biographies. As of 1992, the total number of treatises, historical sources, and memoirs related to journalism history published in periodicals neared 4,000, among which over 1,000 appeared in 56 issues of *News Study Materials* (*Xinwen yanjiu ziliao* 新聞研究資料).

Research on the business of journalism

The attention given to the business of journalism after Reform and Opening Up was reflected by the fact that almost all news units had some form of research on their own business. Some news units also issued publications devoted to such research, apart from engaging in experience exchange activities. Journalism research institutes and societies undertook systematic and in-depth research of the reforms of these news units using new concepts and methodologies.

Research on journalism reform and media legislation

The zealous discussion on journalism reform among various parties involved big questions related to the structure of the newspaper industry, the internal system of newspaper groups, the corporatization of news units, the renewal of the concept of journalism, and the Socialist freedom of the press. With the building of the Socialist legal system, research on media law began to win the auspices of the Party and the government. Beginning with the gathering and publication of materials on media law from other countries, such research looked into theoretical and practical questions particular to China. Organized discussions resulted in internal publications containing research articles that proved conducive to the drafting of China's media law.

Research on foreign journalism and communication studies

Western communication theories reached China in the early 1980s, when the Institute of Journalism Studies of the Chinese Academy of Social Sciences hosted the first symposium on communication studies. The conference provided the principles for understanding and developing communication studies in China: systematic understanding, analytical research, critical absorption, and self-determined innovation. Once the guidelines were given, piles of monographs on the subject were translated and published. In 1986, the Institute held another symposium together with the Department of Journalism of the Remin University of China, pinpointing news communication as the main area of communication research.

Journalism researchers also made great strides in studying the history and present state of journalism in other countries. The most popular research areas were the general history of journalism in the world, and journalism in Western Europe, the United States, and Japan. After the mid-1980s, the changing scenes in the former Soviet Union and Eastern Europe also caused Chinese scholars to pay increasing attention to their journalism work.

Self-identified as part of the Third World, China was particularly concerned about the establishment of the New World Information and Communication Order. In April 1985, the Institute of Journalism Studies of the Chinese Academy of Social Sciences convened the first symposium on the issue. Related articles presented by Chinese researchers became important references for the decision-making of China's missions to the United Nations and specialized institutions of UNESCO.

Research on news audiences

In the past, journalism studies in China had been confined to the theories, business, and history of journalism. News audience research was a new area of study in the Reform and Opening Up era, and it quickly gained recognition domestically and overseas. Modern statistical methods were applied to survey audiences of various media channels. As previously mentioned, the Beijing Journalism Studies Society initiated the first large-scale sampling survey of news audiences in Beijing from June to August 1982, which was joined by the Institute of Journalism Studies of the Chinese Academy of Social Sciences and news units like the *People's Daily*, *Workers' Daily*, and *China Youth Daily*. It was the first time that computer-aided sampling and statistical analysis was used in China, for the integrated study of newspaper, radio, and television audiences. The result was reported by over 20 newspapers and news agencies within and without China. After this, audience surveys and research rapidly developed all over the country. Nationwide surveying became almost an annual activity, while initiatives on a smaller scale continued uninterruptedly throughout the year. Mostly using a sampling method, the surveys collected and analyzed public feedback on news propaganda based

(Cont'd)

on theories and methodologies from communication studies, sociology, social psychology, and statistics, producing practical results that would facilitate the formation of news communication policies.

Works and periodicals on journalism

From the fall of the Gang of Four to the year 1990, China produced a total of approximately 1,380 works on journalism studies, meaning that around 100 works were published every year. This figure was 17.5 times that of the pre-Cultural Revolution era.[36]

As for periodicals on journalism, there were over 100 titles issued by national and provincial-level news units, schools of journalism, journalism organizations, and journalism research institutions in 1989. They included both publicly-circulated and internal publications, either issued nationwide or on a regional basis. At the end of 1990, 26 such journals had obtained a universal *kanhao*. Among the multitude of publications, *China Journalism Yearbook*, which was launched in 1982 with the joint effort of the entire industry, was the most prestigious. At over a million words in length, each volume offered a comprehensive survey of the development of China's news media in the past year, for the reference of journalists, educators, researchers, as well as overseas scholars. See Table 23.11 for some of the prominent journals circulated in this period.

Table 23.11   Major periodicals on journalism in 1989

Journal	Foundation	Frequency of publication
The Press (*Xinwen zhanxian* 新聞戰線)	1956	Monthly
Chinese Journalist (*Zhongguo jizhe* 中國記者)	1987	Monthly
China Journalism Yearbook (*Zhongguo xinwen nianjian* 中國新聞年鑒)	1982	Annual
News Study Materials (*Xinwen yanjiu ziliao* 新聞研究資料)	1979	Quarterly
News Journal (*Xinwen xuekan* 新聞學刊)	1985	Bimonthly
Newsletter of the Beijing Journalism Studies Society (*Xinwen xuehui tongxun* 新聞學會通訊)	1980	Biweekly
China Radio and TV Yearbook (*Zhongguo guangbo dianshi nianjian* 中國廣播電視年鑒)	1986	Annual

Journal	Foundation	Frequency of publication
China Radio and TV Academic Journal (*Zhongguo guangbo dianshi xuekan* 中國廣播電視學刊)	1987	Monthly
News Broadcasting and Television Study (*Xinwen guangbo dianshi yanjiu* 新聞廣播電視研究)	1981	Bimonthly
Journal of Beijing Broadcasting Institute (*Beijing guangbo xueyuan xuebao* 北京廣播學院學報)	1979	Bimonthly
Journal of International Communication (*Guoji xinwen jie* 國際新聞界)	1961	Monthly
Reference for Propagation (*Duiwai xuanchuan cankao* 對外宣傳參考)	1973	Monthly (Biweekly until 1986)
Journalism and Self-Cultivation (新聞與成才 *Xinwen yu chengcai*)	1958 (as *Military Journalist* (*Junshi jizhe* 軍事記者), renamed in 1985)	Monthly
Truth of News (*Xinwen sanmei* 新聞三昧)	1984	Monthly
News and Writing (*Xinwen yu xiezuo* 新聞與寫作)	1984	Monthly
The Journalist Monthly (*Xinwen jizhe* 新聞記者)	1983	Monthly

Sino-foreign academic exchange

Reform and Opening Up opened a new scene for academic exchange on journalism with overseas journalists and scholars. In November 1981, journalists from China and Australia met for the first time at a symposium in Beijing. The conference, where participants gave comments on each other's newspapers, was symbolic as the first occasion of opinion exchange between China's news workers and journalists of a capitalist country. Later, in April 1984, the Symposium on the New World Information and Communication Order in Beijing was welcomed by the presentation of 20 papers from Chinese scholars. As overseas scholars, educators, and journalists flew over to give lectures and attend seminars, China also sent out visiting scholars to partake in academic conferences. Such academic activities not only provided a window for mutual understanding, but also expanded the horizons of journalism research in China.

The modernization of news communications

The modernization of news communications has always been an important issue in journalism reform, for it underpins the improvement of the timeliness, quality, and social benefits of news reporting. Thanks to technological advancement, all kinds of communications experienced rapid modernization in the 1980s. Newspapers, news agencies, radio, and television were all revolutionized.

Newspapers

After a series of modernization efforts during the Reform and Opening Up period, China's newspaper production transitioned from a technologically backward industry at the beginning of the era to an economically efficient high-tech information business in the 1990s.[37]

Phototypesetting

While the West had long been familiar with electronic methods of publishing, including phototypesetting, and Japan had tried its hand at automatic editing and production systems, China did not bring in computer-controlled phototypesetters until the beginning of the 1980s.[38] In 1987, the domestic Hua-Guang (HG) III phototypesetting system produced the first Chinese newspaper to be printed in full sheets. The era of "fire and lead" finally came to an end, as computerized modernity formally took over.

The importation of phototypesetting was initiated by *China Daily*, which acquired equipment from the American Compugraphic Corporation for its startup in June 1981. The English-language newspaper was the first paper in China to benefit from the "cold type" technology and to be sent overseas for printing via Intelsat. In July 1991, it switched to Hewlett-Packard (HP)'s LaserJet printers. The first major Chinese-language newspaper to be phototypeset was the *People's Daily (Overseas Edition)*. It initially adopted a third-generation technology produced by the Japanese Shaken Company, and then upgraded to a fourth-generation system by the American High Technology Solutions (HTS) in 1985. Other newspapers turning to phototypesetting included *Guangming Daily*, *Shanxi Daily (Shanxi ribao 山西日報)*, *Xinjiang Daily (Xinjiang ribao 新疆日報)*, and *Wenhui Bao*.

As importing phototypesetting systems placed a burden on foreign exchange reserves, and most of these systems lacked software tailored for Chinese text, the final solution rested with domestic innovation. In July 1979, the state-owned Weifang

Computer, which was entrusted with the job of prototyping and manufacturing based on the research of Peking University's Institute of Computer Science and Technology, succeeded in printing a tabloid-size sample with its prototype phototypesetting system, the HG I. In September 1983, the HG II for industrial use was released, and it passed the test of stability by printing its first news release for Xinhua in 1985. Thanks to unique Chinese font data compression and regeneration technology, it could support over 10 font types, 16 font sizes, and some 7,000 characters, with extra capacity for supplementary characters. The basic system could be connected to four computer terminals, producing up to 100,000 characters per day. With every addition of a new terminal, the daily capacity could increase by 25,000 characters. Editing could be performed completely at the computer terminals.

This was quickly succeeded by the launch of the even more mature HG III in the year that followed, with which the *Economic Daily* printed the first Chinese newspaper in full sheets. The new system sold a total of 43 copies, to newspaper groups including *Science and Technology Daily* (*Keji ribao* 科技日報), *Workers' Daily*, *People's Liberation Army Daily*, *Shijiazhuang Daily* (*Shijiazhuang ribao* 石家莊日報), *Liaoning Daily*, *Yangtze Daily* (*Changjiang ribao* 長江日報), and *Consumer Times* (*Xiaofei shibao* 消費時報), apart from *Economic Daily*.

In 1987, the Institute of Computer Science and Technology made a groundbreaking achievement with the development of a large-monitor newspaper page management system, which was used to typeset all four pages of the *People's Liberation Army Daily* in March 1989. In August, the *People's Daily* borrowed it to modify the imported HTS system. At about the same time, Weifang's HG IV was introduced into the market in 1988, selling as many as 500 copies in total, with Traditional Chinese versions exported to Hong Kong, Macau, Taiwan, and Singapore. A fifth of the users were newspapers attracted by the low cost and excellent performance of the indigenous system. Its popularization gave impetus to yet another advanced edition, the HG V, which overcame restrictions on font sizes to enable page zooming.

The evolution of the Hua-Guang phototypesetting system coincided with China's general technological and industrial advancement, especially the development of computer technology, in the 1980s. It was also closely related to Wang Yongmin's Wubizixing — or five-stroke character model — input method, which resolved the problem of inputting Chinese text on a computer, and quickly became the standard input method of all newspapers in the country. Outside the Mainland, it was adopted by Hong Kong's *Wenweipo* (*Wenhuibao* 文匯報), Singapore's *Lianhe Zaobao* 聯合早報, and Malaysia's *Nanyang Siang Pau* (*Nanyang shangbao* 南 洋 商 報). To optimize its compatibility with phototypesetting, Wang's Beijing-based software company, Wangma, developed a high-efficiency input machine of improved monitor response times and Traditional/Simplified Chinese conversion in 1990.

Indigenous laser typesetting technology added color to Chinese newspapers in 1992. It was a "Founder" product, which found initial usage in *Macao Daily* (*Aomen ribao* 澳門日報) in January. "Founder" was the newly registered trademark of Beida New Tech, a high-tech venture of Peking University which took the name of Founder Group in 1993. Six months after its first application in Macau, the laser typesetting system engendered the first phototypeset and offset-printed color newspaper on the Chinese Mainland, the *Science and Technology Daily*. The technology enabled full-sheet output that integrated text and color publishing at a resolution of 1,524 lines per inch, reduced printing costs by 70%, and halved typesetting times. In the end, efficiency led to an increase in the content of newspapers in general.

Data transmission and storage

In June 1991, Beida New Tech (Founder) and Weifang Computer had their remote page layout transmission, local area network (LAN), and CD-ROM retrieval systems accredited by the government and launched almost simultaneously. The newspaper industry was about to transform into a high-tech information industry.

Both companies invested in the development of remote page layout transmission technology. Weifang's effort was first brought to fruition, when the *Economic Daily* successfully transmitted all its page layout data to the printing house of *Wenhui Bao* in Shanghai over a long-distance phone line in August 1990. Shortly after that, a similar system was established between the offices of *Wenhui Bao* and the *People's Liberation Army Daily*. In January 1991, Beida New Tech set up an identical system connecting the *Science and Technology Daily* with its printer, *Hubei Daily*, in Wuhan. With the tele-transmission system, the transmission time for a four-page broadsheet was around 45 minutes to an hour.

For efficient long-distance data transmission, Weifang collaborated with the Ministry of Posts and Telecommunications in developing small satellite stations. Also initiated by the *Economic Daily*, the first of these was installed exactly a day before the establishment of the company's tele-transmission system (August 30), at the Guangzhou printing place of *Nanfang Daily*. It took only 6 minutes and 47 seconds to transmit data for a four-page broadsheet, which was then projected onto film for printing. In the following years, the *Economic Daily* extended satellite transmission to its printers in Wuhan and Jinan. Moreover, the *People's Daily* also had advanced satellite stations for page layout transmission built from Hughes Aircraft's equipment.

LANs were the contributions of Beida Founder, which went into operation at the office of the *Science and Technology Daily* in May 1991. Linked to a local network, all microcomputers could be centrally managed without relying on floppy disks for data sharing.

The microcomputer CD-ROM retrieval system, which was more advanced than the microfiche as a means of data storage, again, first appeared at the *Science and Technology Daily* with the support of Beida Founder in January 1991. Permanent storage and quick searching was made possible as an 800 MB disc could hold as many as five to ten years' four-page broadsheets, and a full-text search of 25 million words could be completed in a minute. Moreover, the search results could be displayed on a monitor and printed out from a network printer.

News agencies

In the 1980s and early 1990s, the modernization of the means of communication paved the way for Xinhua's attainment of its goal of being an international news agency. With a huge amount of advanced equipment and technology, it formed a smooth and reliable communications network with substantial data transmission capacity throughout and beyond China.

The broadcast of Chinese-language news to newspaper groups, radio stations, and television stations in the country was an important component of Xinhua's news propaganda. The development of the Chinese-language news distribution system in 1986 marked a leap forward from the facsimile age of the 1950s to the modern era of computer network communications. By the end of 1990, 105 first-class national and provincial newspapers, radio stations, and television stations had been receiving Xinhua releases with microwave circuits and microcomputers, and 65 prefectural news groups had been availing themselves of digital satellite links and microcomputer networks.

To support its expanding international services, Xinhua increased the number of its international communications circuits from 10 in 1983 to 36 in 1986, and then 50 in 1990. The 50 circuits comprised 3 high-speed digital circuits, 2 satellite telephone channels, and more than 40 low-speed telegraph channels. Medium-to-high-speed digital circuits had been set up between Beijing, New York, and Washington; Beijing and Hong Kong, as well as between Beijing and Moscow. In addition, a number of foreign branches were equipped with microcomputer terminals and portable computers, raising the efficiency of news release transmission between the headquarters and branch offices.

The headquarters complex of Xinhua was a key project of the nation's Seventh Five-Year Plan. The building itself was accomplished in September 1989, and the communications project that constituted the nexus of the building was in use from August 1990. Its final inauguration came in December 1990, after government inspection and acceptance.

The use of Xinhua's first portable computer news distribution system at the 10th Asian Games in Seoul in 1986 ended the practice of handwriting news releases in the coverage of major events outside China. Two years later, in the 24th Olympics Games, which also took place in Seoul, news releases in multiple languages were generated and distributed by regions through a modified system. Determined to wrestle with the major news wires from the West, Xinhua managed to outpace news organizations of other countries in 99% of its releases on the Beijing-hosted 11th Asian Games in 1990.

Radio and television

The relative backwardness of radio and television communications rose to be a matter of great concern of the Chinese government in the 1980s. Soon, deficiency led to motivations for remedies. Over the 1980s and early 1990s, a comprehensive broadcast and cable network traversing the whole country was envisioned and brought into reality. Top-down television and radio programs were disseminated from national stations to regional transmitters mainly by satellites, and sometimes by microwaves. From provincial broadcasters down to local stations, microwaves were the major means of transmission, which was supplemented by broadcast translators. Local programs were transmitted bottom-up to Beijing also mostly via microwave links. Television coverage was simultaneously supported by satellite and cable networks. The swift transformation of radio and television services after Reform and Opening Up was consummated at the 1990 Beijing Asian Games, where communications technologies were tested against the demands of a fast-paced international event.

Communications satellites

In November 1988, CCTV started migrating its first and second nationwide programs from the rented Intelsat satellite onto the second domestically-built operational communications satellite. As for the first indigenous innovation, it was used to deliver the first three nationwide programs by the Central People's

Broadcasting Station and China Radio International. With these satellites, broadcast relay stations were supplied with quality program signals.

Following in the footsteps of CCTV, Xinjiang, Yuennan, Guizhou, and Tibet began delivering local radio and television programs within their administrative divisions by communications satellites in the year that followed. This prompted the building of satellite relay and receiving stations across the country. By the end of 1990, over 19,000 earth stations had been established, in which 10,780 could relay signals and 8,725 simply received radio waves. The launching of communications satellites eventually facilitated the development of television relay stations. In 1990 alone, 2,574 such stations were built, making the total number 24,713. There were 31,278 television transmitters in the country, serving 80% of the national population.

Microwave links

The building of a national microwave network took off in the 1980s, with the addition of provincial links to the Ministry of Posts and Telecommunications' national links. The network supported the delivery of the majority of provincial-level television programs to counties and cities, as well as the transmission of most shows of major local events back to the provincial capitals and Beijing. By the end of 1989, 1,401 microwave relay stations had been constructed, and the total length of all microwave links spanned 45,388 kilometers.

Broadcast translators

Broadcast translators were set up to rebroadcast FM and television signals on other frequencies. Although communications satellites bore an increasing role in relaying radio and television signals, television translators continued to be an important means of television coverage. Moreover, the development of broadcast translators for relaying stereo FM signals gradually extended the coverage of FM radio.

Cable networks

For a long time, geographical barriers like seas and deserts had prevented the formation of countywide cable radio networks in some parts of rural China. The solution found in 1984 was the building of low-power FM radio stations. Apart from relaying programming for town/township-level radio and television stations, they also provided direct FM radio services within the county seats. By the end of 1988, 328 county-level FM stations had been established. Radio reception in rural areas benefited greatly from this integration of cable and wireless technologies.

According to figures at the end of 1990, there were 3,011 county-level radio stations in the whole country. At or below the township level, broadcast links extended over 627,931 kilometers, and a total of 82,216,000 home speakers penetrated 37.3% of the rural households. The rate of village access to radio broadcasts was 69.9%.

In a few years' time, cable television evolved from a rarity at the beginning of the 1980s into a common system for distributing television programming, as community antennas originally built for improving the quality of television reception provided the basis for an extensive cable television network. Its pace of development went far ahead of expectations. At the end of 1989, the number of households equipped with cable television already approached eight million, leading to estimates that there would be an annual addition of three million in the years to come.

Other technologies

Color television reached China in January 1988, with the completion of the China Central Television Building, which was also known, significantly, as the CCTV Central Color TV Center. The center had a computer-controlled local network that connected the systems and devices for broadcasting, production, and business management. For program broadcasting in particular, there was a computerized transmission control room that could air four programs at a time, and news centers equipped with production studios and videotape editing rooms. The final point of transmission was the master control room, where all audio and video signals were sent over microwave links or to satellite uplink stations.

Electronic news-gathering (ENG) devices, which entered China in 1980, were crucial to the improvement of the timeliness of news coverage. With the introduction of ENG cameras and recorders together with electronic editors, the lag between the capture of footage and broadcasts was shortened. News production was sped up.

The 1990 Beijing Asian Games

In 1990, a series of television communications facilities were built especially for the coverage of the Beijing Asian Games, with which the host country was eager to impress international spectators. These included a 385-meter Central Television Tower, an International Radio and Television News Center, supporting facilities in the Long-Distance Telephone Building, the CCTV Building, and the Broadcasting Building, as well as broadcasting equipment in each of the 31 sports venues. All communications devices were some of the most advanced technologies of the 1980s.

Television live broadcasts were performed in 19 of the 31 venues during the Games. The 19 venues had a total of 50 sets of microwave transmission equipment, allowing 14 video signals to be simultaneously transmitted to the International Radio and Television News Center, with half of the quota being reserved for foreign news organizations. In the rest of the venues, electronic field production (EFP) and ENG devices were employed to record events. Footage was dispatched to the International Radio and Television News Center and the CCTV Building to be pro-produced into integrated shows for the use of foreign television companies. In addition, the Central People's Broadcasting Station and China Radio International also made live broadcasts in the major sports venues.

All post-production work was done in the Broadcasting Building, the CCTV Building, and the International Radio and Television News Center. CCTV transmitted the first two shows from the Long-Distance Telephone Building via microwave links and satellites, and the third show directly from its headquarters. The Central People's Broadcasting Station sent the signals of its six shows to transmission stations all over the country via cables, microwaves, and satellites. China Radio International's shows, which were available in 38 foreign languages, Mandarin, and other Chinese dialects, were sent through the same means to transmission stations outside China. The smooth operation of radio and television communications during the Beijing Games was a symbolic mark of technological advancement.

Notes

Chapter 23

1. **Fengqing** was a 10,000-ton freighter designed and built in China, which made a successful voyage to Romania from Shanghai in 1974. The Gang of Four then hyped it up as exemplary proof of domestic shipbuilding, attacking Zhou and Deng for their preference for buying ships abroad and their servitude to things foreign.

2. The movement of "Admiring the Legalists and Criticizing the Confucians" (*ping fa pi ru* 評法批儒) was propelled along the line of the Campaign to Criticize Lin Biao and Confucius. Manipulating the opposition between Legalism and Confucianism in traditional Chinese culture, the Gang of Four attempted to legitimize the authority of Jiang Qing by drawing a parallel between Jiang and the Han Empress Lü Zhi, who supposedly ruled by Legalism, while condemning Confucianism, to which Premier Zhou was associated.

3. China's university admission system was reformed in 1973, leading to the resumption of admission examinations that summer. A former Red Guard, Zhang Tiesheng was among the prospective students sitting for the exam, who, however, was unable to answer the questions. Yet, instead of turning in a blank answer sheet, he wrote the "Letter to the Revered Leaders" that made him the so-called "blank answer sheet hero" hailed by the Gang of Four, where he ascribed his failure to study to his devotion to collective farm work.

4. Written by a Primary Five girl called Huang Shuai, the letter and diaries mainly recorded general everyday conflicts between teachers and students, but they were manipulated by Chi Qun and Xie Jingyi to portray the prototype of an anti-traditionalist hero.

5. During the Cultural Revolution, university graduates were motivated to return to the farm, following the experience of the Chaoyang Agricultural University.

6. The large markets (*daji* 大集) of Ha'ertao epitomized the Socialist large markets, which forced owners of private vegetable farms and private plots to submit all yields to a centralized supply and marketing cooperative to be sold at fixed prices, in order to eradicate all elements of capitalism.

7. Wang Yazhuo 王亞卓 was the penname adopted by Xingzhuo, which comprised a character from the names of Xing (Zhuo 卓) and his two friends, Wang Wenyao (Wang 王) and En Yali (Ya 亞). Having read the "A Letter and Diary Abstracts from A Primary School Student," the three of them decided to write the school girl a letter pointing out the blind spots of her "anti-traditionalist" attitude, which ended up inviting political criticism.

8. CCCPC Party Literature Research Office 中共中央文獻研究室, *Guanyu jianguo yilai dang de ruogan lishi wenti de jueyi zhushi ben (xiuding)* 關於建國以來黨的若干歷史問題的決議注釋本（修訂）(Annotated Resolution on Certain Historical Questions of the Party Since the Foundation of the People's Republic of China [Amended]) (Beijing: People's Publishing House, 1985), 476–77.

9. "Deng fu zhuxi zai quan jun zhengzhi gongzuo huiyi shang de jianghua (Yijiuqiba nian liu yue er ri)" 鄧副主席在全軍政治工作會議上的講話（一九七八年六月二日）(Vice President Deng's Speech at the All-Army Conference on Political Work [June 2, 1978]), *Renmin ribao* 人民日報 (People's Daily), June 6, 1978. Translation taken from Deng Xiaoping, *Selected Works of Deng Xiaoping*, vol. 2 (Beijing: Foreign Languages Press, 1984).

10. CCCPC Party Literature Research Office 中共中央文獻研究室, *Guanyu jianguo yilai dang de ruogan lishi wenti de jueyi zhushi ben (xiuding)* 關於建國以來黨的若干歷史問題的決議注釋本（修訂）(Annotated Resolution on Certain Historical Questions of the Party Since the Foundation of the People's Republic of China [Amended]),(Beijing: People's Publishing House, 1985), 480–81. Translation

taken from Deng Xiaoping, *Selected Works of Deng Xiaoping*, vol. 2 (Beijing: Foreign Languages Press, 1984).

11. Ibid.

12. The victims of the incident were managers of a youth shop in Shuangcheng County, Heilongjiang, who made a large purchase of washing machines from Beijing. When the machines arrived at the Shangchengbao Railway Station, the railway staff in charge of the unloading demanded buying 10 of them at the wholesale price, and retaliated by destroying the goods upon the managers' rejection. As a result, all the washing machines were destroyed or damaged.

13. The Lubuge Hydroelectric Project was China's first attempt of building a hydroelectric station by international bidding with a loan from the World Bank.

14. *Zhongguo gongchandang di shi'er ci quanguo daibiao dahui wenjian huibian* 中國共產黨第十二次全國代表大會文件彙編 (Collection of Documents from the 12th National Congress of the CPC) (Beijing: People's Publishing House, 1982), 28.

15. The paper had another editorial about the hero, titled "On Lei Feng," back in 1963.

16. The Hua Shan rescue team was made up of students of the Fourth Military Medical University, who, while hiking in Mount Hua, volunteered to rescue some ten tourists who fell off a cliff by accident.

17. Originally a small and isolated village-town in Xiyang County, Shanxi, Dazhai became the agricultural model by which production could multiply by observing the Party's line since Mao proclaimed the slogan "In Agriculture learn from Dazhai" in 1964.

18. *Zhongguo xinwen nianjian* 中國新聞年鑒 (China Journalism Yearbook) (Beijing: Zhongguo xinwen chubenshe, 1983), 260.

19. Ibid. 186, 200.

20. Ibid.

21. Ibid., 24.

22. *Makesi zhuyi xinwen gongzuo wenxian xuandu* 馬克思主義新聞工作文獻選讀 (Selected Readings from Marxist Works on Journalism) (Beijing: People's Publishing House, 1990), 243.

23. "Zai jiejian shoudu jieyan budui jun yishang ganbu shi de jianghua" 在接見首都戒嚴部隊軍以上幹部時的講話 (Address to Officials at or above the Rank of General in Command of the Troops Enforcing Martial Law in Beijing), *Renmin ribao* 人民日報 (**People's Daily**), June 28, 1989. Translation taken from Deng Xiaoping, *Selected Works of Deng Xiaoping*, vol. 2 (Beijing: Foreign Languages Press, 1984).

24. The concept borrowed from Soviet Russia, the so-called Children's Palaces, or *Shaoniangong*, in China are first-grade after-school venues housed in palace-like establishments (or sometimes historical palaces) that provide educational and leisure activities. The term also refers to organizations running these venues.

25. Combined reporting (*zuhe baodao* 組合報導) was in fact a combination of various presentation forms that were employed to uncover an event from manifold perspectives.

26. Wang Qianghua 王強華, "Xinwen guanli he baokan fanrong" 新聞管理和報刊繁榮 (The Management of the News Industry and the Prosperity of News Publications), *Xinwen zhanxian* 新聞戰線 (The Press) (5) (1992).

27. *Makesi zhuyi xinwen gongzuo wenxian xuandu* 馬克思主義新聞工作文獻選讀 (Selected Readings from Marxist Works on Journalism) (Beijing: People's Publishing House, 1990), 243.

28. The "coastal open cities" referred to coastal cities opened to foreign investment succeeding the establishment of the first Special Economic Zones in 1980. Dalian, Qinhuangdao, Tianjin, Yantai, Qingdao, Lianyungang, Nantong, Shanghai, Ningbo, Wenzhou, Fuzhou, Guangzhou, Zhanjiang, and Beihai were opened in 1984. In 1985, the economically open areas were further expanded.

29. In terms of geographical distribution, 15 came from Asia, 12 Latin America, 10 Africa, 7 Europe and the United States, and 4 Middle East.

30. See P.26 for the radio station's coverage of the unloading incident at the Shuangchengbao Railway Station.

31. The incident took place in the midst of a propaganda war across the strait. In the incident, Wang Xijue defected to Guangzhou while flying the freighter from Bangkok to Hong Kong. According to Xinhua, Wong's attempt was to reunite with his relatives in Mainland China. In the end, Taiwan was forced to send envoys to negotiate with China, which agreed on the return of the plane on the condition of the lifting of the Three No's policy.

32. Fang Kejing 方可靜, "Qian tan xinwen sheying de gaige he chuangxin — jian yu hu wugong tongzhi shangque" 淺談新聞攝影的改革和創新 — 兼與胡武功同志商榷 (A Brief Discussion of the Reform and Innovations of Photojournalism — and an Argument with Comrade Hu Wugong), *Shanghai xinwen sheying xuehui tongxun* 上海新聞攝影學會通訊 (Bulletin of Shanghai Photojournalism Society), July 15, 1986.

33. Hu Wugong 胡武功, "Guanyu 'chuzheng' zhenglun de sikao — jian da fang ke jing tongzhi" 關於《出征》爭論的思考 — 兼答方可靜同志 (Reflections on the Debate over Expedition — and a Response to Comrade Fang Kejing), *Xinwen shying* 新聞攝影 (News Photography) (11), 1986.

34. Wang Qianghua 王強華, "Xinwen guanli he baokan fanrong" 新聞管理和報刊繁榮 (News Management and the Prosperity of News Publications), *Xinwen zhanxian* 新聞戰線 (The Press)(5) (1992).

35. The journalist was An Ke of Radio Guangdong.

36. The figure has been compiled based on the section "Works on Chinese Journalism" in *Zhongguo xinwen nianjian* (**China Journalism Yearbook** 中國新聞年鑑) of 1982 to 1991.

37. Min Dahong 閔大洪, "Woguo baoye jishu de huashidai bianhua" 我國報業技術的劃時代變化 (The Epochal Changes of China's Newspaper Technology), *Xinwen yanjiu ziliao* 新聞研究資料 (News Study Materials)(2)(1992) details the technological changes in China's newspaper industry.

38. *The Nikkei* (*Nihon Keizai Shimbun* 日本経済新聞) became the world's first newspaper produced entirely by computer editing in 1971.

Index

All-China Journalists Association 115, 118-19, 125, 127

Beijing Daily 7-8, 19, 28
Beijing Journalism Studies Society 18, 37, 109, 118, 120-2, 130-1
bourgeois liberalism 2, 16, 45-7, 49
businesses, news-related 56-7, 77, 83-6

Capital Journalism Studies Society 107, 118, 120
CCTV (China Central Television) 30, 37, 39, 47, 50, 52, 63, 97-100, 102-5, 117, 127, 137-8, 140
Central Broadcasting Bureau 4, 88, 99-100, 117
Central People's Broadcasting Station 12, 25-6, 30-1, 34, 37, 39, 41, 50-1, 89-91, 93, 96, 98-9, 117, 127, 140
Central People's Broadcasting Station (Taiwan Service) 39, 41
China Central Television. See CCTV
China Daily 39, 41, 55, 62, 76, 107, 133
China News Service 39-41, 86-7
China Radio International (CRI) 37-9, 41, 51, 96-7, 117, 127, 140
China Youth Daily 15, 18, 26, 28, 34, 51, 60, 130
Conference, National Broadcasting Work 87-8, 99, 117
Conference, National Radio and Television Work 88, 100, 117
CPC Propaganda Department 21, 114-15, 123, 125-6
critical journalism 26, 29, 32-3, 49, 91, 99, 104-5, 108

Cultural Revolution 2-3, 7, 12, 18-20, 28, 32-3, 37, 43, 60, 64, 74, 78, 87, 91, 128

Deng Xiaoping 3, 7-8, 10-14, 21, 27, 42, 45, 48, 58, 92, 122, 141-2
documentaries 98, 110-12

Economic Daily 25-6, 63, 125, 134-5
Economic news 21, 23-7, 40, 51, 74, 104, 121. See also newspapers, economic
economic reform 25-7, 34-5, 43-4, 49, 51, 56, 58, 74, 119
electronic news-gathering (ENG) 98, 139

Gang of Four 2-11, 13-20, 45, 90, 122, 128, 131, 141
Guangdong Television 101-4
Guangming Daily 3, 6, 12-13, 17-18, 29, 62, 127, 133

Hua Guofeng 2, 9, 10

international audiences, news for 36, 39-42, 79, 88-9, 113

journalism education 2, 121-3, 125-6
journalism research 2, 21, 106, 125, 127-30, 132
journalism societies 118, 120-2
journalism theory 8, 18, 47-8, 126-8

Liberation Daily 4, 6-7, 129
Lin Biao 2-4, 6, 8, 11, 14, 16-20, 128

Mao Zedong 3, 6, 10, 15, 111, 121, 128, 142
Ministry of Radio, Film, and Television 114-17

Ministry of Radio and Television   88-9, 93, 100, 117

newspapers
  categories of 53-73
  children's and teens' 59-60
  economic 58
  educational 58-9
  English-language 55, 62, 133
  enterprise 65
  ethnic minority 54, 58, 60-2, 64-72
  evening 64
  for overseas Chinese 61-2
  legal 30, 54-5, 59, 68
  official CPC 54-6, 63, 66, 76
  radio and television 62-3, 69
  science and technology 31, 54-5, 58
  senior 59-60
  service 62-4
  weekend 63
  women's 54, 60
newsreels 97, 110

People's Daily   3-15, 18-20, 22-8, 33-5, 37, 47, 50-1, 61, 63, 75, 107, 115, 127, 130, 134
People's Daily (Overseas Edition)   39, 40-2, 76, 133
People's Liberation Army Daily   3, 7, 9-10, 13-14, 19, 49, 61, 63, 134-5
photojournalism 2, 106-10, 124

radio, cable 88-9, 96, 138
radio programs 31, 41, 87-97
  art and literature 93, 94
  commentary 90, 94
  economic 90, 95
  educational 92
  ethnic minority 93, 96

for children and youth 92, 95
for Taiwan 93, 96
interactive 92
music 95
news 92, 94-5
on theoretical education 89-90, 94
overseas. See China Radio International (CRI).
Reference News 37, 61-2, 85-6
Reform and Opening Up   28, 37, 39-40, 43, 50-1, 57-8, 60, 65-6, 74-6, 79-80, 83-4, 110-11, 116-17, 128-30, 132-3

satellite   37, 39, 76, 82-3, 88-9, 97-100, 135-40
Shanghai Television 101-3
Socialism 11, 17, 20, 24-5, 28, 43, 45-6, 48
Socialist spiritual civilization 2, 27-8, 30, 33
State Press and Publication Administration   53-4, 56, 114-16

Taiwan   37-9, 41-3, 76, 86-7, 92-3, 96, 112, 119, 134, 143
technology, news   76-8, 81, 83-4, 86, 96-8, 103-4, 135-7, 139
television news 88, 97-105
television programs, other 31, 106

Third Plenary Session of the 11th CPC Central Committee   2, 9, 11, 16, 18-19, 21-4, 30, 34-5, 42, 46, 52, 57-8, 61, 108-11, 127
Tiananmen Incident, 1976 7, 10, 15
Tiananmen Square protests, 1989 40, 47-50
truth, criterion of 3, 9-10, 12-15, 17, 89
Two Whatevers 9-11, 13-15

Workers' Daily 15, 18, 25, 33, 35, 61, 109, 126-7, 130, 134 world news 36-7, 74, 79, 84, 98-101, 124

Xinhua 4-6, 8, 13-15, 18, 21, 33, 37-9, 50,
     74-5, 77-87, 98, 109, 115, 126-7, 136-7
Xinwen Lianbo 37, 50, 98-100

Zhou Enlai, Premier 4-5, 141

CPSIA information can be obtained at www.ICGtesting.com
Printed in the USA
BVOW07*0801040614

355321BV00003B/24/P

9 789814 332330